ANXIETY IS NO FUN!

A HOLISTIC APPROACH TO OVERCOME IT

AURA JADDEE, CHT, LMT

PALM AND LOTUS PUBLISHING

Published by Palm and Lotus Publishing

www.palmandlotus.com

ISBN: 979-8-9851252-5-2

Dedicated to:
All the brave souls
who desperately want to
feel FREE from anxiety.

KNOW THIS: If you picked up this book you are halfway there, because what you are seeking is seeking you! You are loved!

P.S. – There is nothing wrong with you!

CONTENTS

Disclaimer

The information and advice herein is not intended to replace the services of trained health professionals or serve as a substitute for medical advice. You are advised to consult your health care professional with regard to matters relating to your health, and in particular, regarding matters that may require diagnosis or medical attention. None of these recommendations have been evaluated by the FDA, nor are they intended to diagnose, treat, or cure any disease. The author assumes no risk.

This book is for **Educational Purposes Only.**
As the author, I am only sharing what worked for me. The action you take based on this book is solely your risk and responsibility. Everyone's healing journey is unique.

Aura Jaddee

INTRODUCTION

This book. It was not in my original plan to write this as my first book. Instead, I was working on a cookbook. I love food! But, this book kept coming up to the surface of my consciousness and making itself known that it was meant to be written. At first, I taught it as a class, but then I thought, "No! More people need to know this!" It was meant to be written first, and as I've written this book, it has corresponded well to the healing journey I've been on for the last fourteen years. As I write this book, it's like the closing of a chapter of my life that took determination and belief in something much, much better. I'm so grateful that I wrote this book, so grateful that I went through it...but also so glad to be done.

As a massage therapist, I've seen many people on my table who are stuck in the darkness of constant anxiety. I recognize it quickly, because I know what it feels like. I either pick up on their anxiety prior to their arrival, or it vibrates off them as they lay there so desperately wanting calm.

The cover of this book is what so many deeply desire— relaxation of mind, body, and soul. You'll notice with the cover art that the sunset is part in the shadow of darkness and the other, still in the light. It's how you might feel when you are in the pit of anxiety—you feel half controlled by it (the shadow side), while the other half feels like your true self, still holding on to hope.

Some of you might have had this book on your shelf for a while before actually reading it. Others may have been aware of this book or heard me talk about it on social media for a while before purchasing it. For some of you, you knew immediately that you had to have this book. Some of you might have come here as the latter part of your healing journey. You have danced around the white elephant in the room and can now heal your anxiety from a good place. Maybe you have healed enough of the contributing factors that this focal point has greatly diminished—outstanding! Perhaps you simply jumped in hot with both feet—sick and tired of feeling this way. However it is that you came across this book, it was the perfect time for each of you. Whatever path you took to get here, will ultimately lead you home.

With this book, I don't get into the science behind all the factors contributing to anxiety; I am simply putting tools into your hands. It is your responsibility to, then, look further into each health tip if it resonates with you. I've discovered, over the years, how much humans lean on professionals to tell them what to do with their bodies instead of discovering how to listen to their own perfectly-tuned inner guidance. I've learned not to put people down for having a lack of awareness of their own bodies, but rather, to point out how much they actually *do* understand. I try to draw out what they already know, which tends to be a lot more than they realize. Then, instead of becoming just another crutch by doing it all for them, I give them the information and the homework that enables them to put their health where it belongs—in their hands. Even the medical field will agree that you must be your own best health advocate.

In this book you will find sixty-six ways to help you overcome anxiety in a holistic manner. Holistic, meaning in a natural way, a whole-body and a whole-being approach. In other words, everything is connected—body, mind, and soul. Every single tip I talk about I have, indeed, incorporated into my life to help overcome anxiety. In general, I only like to share or help on topics that I have actual experience with.

The sections in this book are set up in the order that I healed—physical before emotional/energetic. The physical aspects were what I understood initially, but the more I healed, the more I truly understood the emotional/energetic aspects and how they are all connected.

Everyone's experience and origin of anxiety is different. What I've discovered is that it is a multifaceted issue, with physical, emotional, and energetic components. There might be an obvious cause—a result of trauma, for example—or it might have been something that was slowly brewing below the surface. It could be a combination of factors; perhaps it was brewing, but then there was that last drop in the bucket that made it overflow. Or just a single traumatic experience and then how your body handled it physically and emotionally afterwards.

The spiral of not being able to think or function well with anxiety keeps you operating in survival mode – not much thriving is going on. HOWEVER, to overcome anxiety, you have to choose to step away from it in your mind and face it head on, which can be super difficult at first. I started by examining the anxiety and asking some basic questions: Where did the anxiety start? What do I know about it thus far? How does this make me feel? I started to unpack the vortex that was sucking me down. Then, I was able to be calm enough to begin to identify what was truly going on.

At the end of each chapter in the book are self-reflection questions. Do them! Invest in yourself. That's where the change happens.

And, I urge you to read the dedication...and then re-read it again and again.

Aura Jaddee

PART I

THE PHYSICAL

Remember, as you "clean house" (i.e., get rid of toxins, memories, conditions, trauma) the dust will be stirred up. At first, the house will seem dirtier before the dust settles. Afterwards, though, the house is clean and you feel better—similar to any healing journey.

Because your anxiety can have multiple layers to it, utilizing a multi-faceted approach can really help to address all angles. Some people stress out about doing too many things at once, such that they won't know which thing helped. First, trust yourself—you'll know what is working and/or what combinations of interventions work best for you. Second, why wait? Take a multi-faceted approach and hit the physical and emotional/energetic all at once.

Little did I know, in the beginning, that the physical manifestations that were so present were actually a representation of the deeper, darker control that was under the surface.

People who knew me before my anxiety would have said that I was super healthy. And yes, on the surface, it looked that way; I ate a paleo diet, practiced proper food combining, and engaged in vegetable juicing, enemas, regular lymphatic drainage massage, and more. However, no amount of healthy practices will negate burnout. It will not prevent the initiation of a healing journey, on any level, when the time has come.

How important is it for you to feel better?

What can you let go of to create space, to allow more money for your self-care, to allot more time, to have a greater sense of calm in your life?

As you prioritize *yourself* and let go of the things and people that weigh you down, you will be surprised how free and calm you feel through the de-cluttering of your energy. The more you simplify, the better you will feel.

Health doesn't happen on its own, and a lack of illness doesn't equate health. Things can brew under the surface for many years before becoming a noticeable problem. Self-care IS healthcare.

For more information on the health tips found in this book, please visit the Resource section in the back.

1

THE BACKSTORY AND THE CRACKING OPEN

Sometimes, a "cracking open" is the best thing that can ever happen to you. To this day, I am incredibly grateful for that experience, as it redirected my life and saved me from the suppression of myself...where any remnant of *me* was wiped away.

I was a quiet little girl, the middle child in a large religious family, who liked to be happy in my imaginary world. I understood what was going on around me and didn't need spoken words to function. I often preferred to stay to myself. I was not concerned about social or developmental norms that were expected and wasn't speaking much or communicating like the other kids. Therefore, I was sent, daily, to a language development school from the age of two until kindergarten. As I got older, I went to the special help classes at school until I eventually outgrew this non-communication issue.

From a young age, I received the message that there was something wrong with me; this came from both within my home and the religion in which I was raised. Whenever I tried to express my true self, or start to explore, or act on my dreams, desires, or goals, there would be some sort of smackdown—an explanation of why it was wrong, or not allowed—after which, some sort of control mechanism would be put in place to override or replace what I wanted.

Religious Abuse

I come from a background of religious abuse. Religious abuse is controlling another person, through the threat of hell, if they don't believe, behave, or live a certain way. It's their way or hell. No other ideas, thoughts, actions, suggestions, desires, goals, dreams, or conversations are allowed. They seem to delight in your soul being troubled. Read that last sentence again. My family read the bible daily and went to church three times a week. No swearing, no lying, no sex outside of marriage, no drinking, no smoking, no drugs, no dating or marrying others outside of the church, no ungodly music. I had to be careful who my friends were. There was no dancing; I'd even have to leave a wedding early if they started dancing. Pretty much no real living, no allowance to be oneself...just following their religious rules.

In my case, I was also told that I couldn't go into music. My true essence was as a creative; in fact, this book is an expression of that creativity! Instead, I was talked into massage therapy training and providing holistic body-work within the Amish community. Even more, I hated being controlled in this way. To those in the religion, this way of living and believing was the *only* right way, and everything else was a fear or sin. I believe religious abuse is much more prevalent than people realize or talk about. I hated working with the Amish, because they practice yet another form of religious abuse, and it was mirroring back to me exactly what I was experiencing in my own life.

How do you let go of religious abuse? Forgive, heal the many layers, and understand that those who perpetuate these ideas believe it is the best way to live. For many, it is all they have ever known.

Narcissist Control

Narcissistic control was also occurring in my family, in combination with the religious abuse. For me, it was this kind of quiet, abusive control where the controller *appeared* loving and healing to others but delighted in whatever aliment I would get. They seemed to be jealous of my success and very afraid that I would be better than them at anything. They never wanted me to do well or to think for myself. They enjoyed getting me to do things they knew I hated or things that weren't my idea; they would give me gifts they knew I didn't like. They'd hold grudges for years—even though forgiveness was talked about in the religion, it was never demonstrated. If I wanted to participate in something that might demonstrate talent or went against the bible, I was told no; afterwards, however, I might be given a version of it back to me. It was not allowed unless it was their way. It was really warped and confusing. In some ways it was as if they wanted to make me a carbon copy of them, as long as I was not any better than them. I was definitely not allowed to be myself.

I was always given the silent treatment. When I would say something, they would stare at me with a weird look on their face and not respond. This happened over and over and over again. Ironically, there was enormous push to get me to communicate when I was a child; yet, whenever I would say anything, they would ignore me, as if I wasn't there. Their silence reinforced that there was something wrong with me, that what I had to say didn't matter—therefore, I did not matter. I had no voice either way. They enjoyed using my energy for their benefit (like getting me to work with the Amish to "help" them). They would hiss in my ear that, because I liked to hum or occasionally talk to myself, I would end up with mental health issues and take my own life! I now understand that those comments were a twisted representation of their own self-talk.

Remember that how others treat you reflects *their* own inner story and trauma.

When you are being abused, you often have NO idea that it is going on. It's not until another perspective is shown to you that you can look back and realize what was happening and that none of it was healthy. Music was my therapy to help me feel my feelings, to soothe my energetic and emotional well-being. Music put me in a better vibration, and helped me escape the suffocation.

It's very important to recognize if you're being abused. One way to tell is to ask yourself, "Is my life looking exactly like somebody else would prefer it to be?"

"No one can throw a bigger tantrum than a narcissist who's losing control of someone else's mind."

- **Author unknown**

The Cracking Open

I remember I was driving to college. I'd been having some underlying anxiety but didn't realize it. Partway to college, out of nowhere, I literally felt like I was dying. It was a full-on panic attack. Looking back, it felt as if someone was angrily crushing my heart or had ripped an energetic attachment out of my soul. While writing this book, I've really examined the energy around that moment. It felt like someone was heatedly saying to me, while yanking me back on the chain, "How dare you try to be better than me?!" I had never had a panic attack before, so I had no idea what was happening in that moment, but I knew I couldn't continue. I quickly made an illegal U-turn on the highway and returned home.

I remember laying on the couch, wondering if I was going to die. That feeling of dying eventually went away, but I proceeded to have PTSD in the form of major anxiety that would come out of nowhere again, and that feeling would return. This fear would cripple me; I would get so filled with anxiety that I didn't want to leave the house...as if I were literally chained there. This moment was my "cracking open." It seemed like the universe had broken the dam on what my life had been. Everything was being thrust into my face like a giant dust ball for me to examine. It was painful, yes, but ultimately, it was the gateway to freedom.

Prior to this setback, my plan had been to go to college for a pre-medicine degree so I could move to the West Coast and earn my Naturopathic Doctorate. But the universe knew that that plan was NOT my true essence; instead, it sent me this traumatic experience as a redirection. And, the change in my path was all based on trusting my intuition. Since then, I've realized that I am not a healer, I am a creator. Yes, I was conditioned to be a great healer, but it was never my true self. What I've also learned is that, although I could have completed this book sooner, the universe wanted me to go through a bit more healing and some massive letting go (narcissistic release), because otherwise, this book would have taken on an unhealed tone.

Line in the Sand

Dark hole, line in the sand. The anxiety was new to me; I didn't know what it was. I had started to take minerals —the fear of having another panic attack was over-whelming! I felt like I was being sucked down into a dark hole, and I didn't like it. Feeling down and dark was not my nature. One day, I had simply had enough of it! I put my foot down and said to myself, "From here on out, I am ONLY GOING TO GET BETTER!" I mentally drew a line in the sand that day, and with a VERY determined attitude, I set out to get better, find answers, and be happy!

After that dark hole, line in the sand moment, I decided to get counseling. I went five times, after which the counselor proclaimed that I was better and didn't have to go anymore. I certainly didn't feel better, but I was glad *she* thought so, because that gave me hope. At least I was going out visiting people, shopping, and driving myself instead of being at home.

Looking back, I am incredibly grateful that the universe cracked me open and sent me on a healing journey. It was the start of a new road and approach to life.

Diving into the dark to heal doesn't sound fun. But remember, the sun shines on everything, and the moonlight only illuminates what is true.

Self-Reflection

1. What was your "cracking open" point?
2. What made you stop dead in your tracks?
3. What made you feel trapped?
4. Are you grateful for it now?
5. Take some time to briefly write out your story. Sometimes, it is helpful to have a timeline so you can get a better understanding of who you are, what makes you *you*, and when and where the anxiety started. It could even just be one-line sentences for each period of your life.

2

_____

SAVING MYSELF

When my anxiety first surfaced, I didn't understand all the pieces or its multi-layered nature; I thought it was just stress and burn out. And, being a holistically-minded woman, I did not seek a traditional medical doctor to figure out the anxiety. Instead, I piecemealed a treatment plan for myself, figuring it out as I went along.

I had never experienced anxiety before, so I didn't even know what that was. I knew what nervousness was. For me, that was more situational, something that would happen before a stressful event, such as a piano recital, driver's license exam, or school test...where you feel nervous right before you start it, then it subsides. With nervousness you can experience an upset stomach or a pounding heart; however, with anxiety, it felt like an irrational, mind-controlling fear.

Living in fear is how I would describe my anxiety. I was constantly worried that I would have another panic attack, and I was terrified of that possibility. I also found myself overwhelmed by EVERYTHING. I remember one instance when I freaked out that, *if I couldn't get my knee-high boots off, I would have a panic attack!* The reason I remember this so clearly is because my next thought was, "This is so ridiculous! You will get your boots off with no issues and no panic attack." I realized then that I needed to start working on it. It was PTSD.

Little did I know, at that time, that by following my strong desire to be free from anxiety, I would ultimately be saving myself.

Adrenal Fatigue

I remember pulling a super thick, holistic, health-based encyclopedia off the bookshelf and paging through the various conditions, searching for the cause of my anxiety. I came across adrenal fatigue, and it seemed to describe exactly what I was going through. I was attending college by that time, taking a full course load and working. Around the same time, a close friend moved away, my work situation was changing, and—

underlying all of that—I had been unknowingly holding myself "on guard" for twenty-eight years of my life. That hidden tendency was a protective mechanism based on my upbringing. My adrenal glands were shot. I now had a good understanding of what was going on with me physically.

Adrenal fatigue occurs when your adrenal glands are taxed out from constant tension, stress, fear, or suppression over a long period of time. This can lead to a relentless cycle of fear, worry, doubt, fight or flight, or burnout—the unhealthy version of your adrenal glands. You may even develop fears over relatively minor things. The adrenals are about safety. If you don't feel safe, then your adrenal glands will be on high alert all the time, subconsciously.

What can you do to feel safe? What do you have to acknowledge, to face, to confront now or in the past in order to feel safe? Sometimes, the fear of facing an old wound can make you dance around it, but truly, avoiding it is worse than acknowledging it. I know from experience how freeing it is to sit down, write out your feelings, and let ALL the emotions come out. For example, "You hurt me when_____." Really allow yourself to feel those emotions. And then end it with, "I forgive you." You can rip up the paper afterwards, throw it into the river or ocean, freeze it, or burn it. But allow yourself to utterly and completely release it.

You might feel physically sick after releasing or letting go in this way or having been through a stressful situation. When we release something we've carried for a long time, our adrenal glands relax and no longer have to be in fight mode. But then, what often happens is that the rest of the body lets you know how taxed it was during this timeframe, causing you to feel physically sick or a bit off as you recover.

This happened while I was studying for both my massage state board and my massage finals at the same time—I took them ten days apart. I remember feeling exhausted for six weeks afterwards, even though I was no longer under the stress of school and finals. In another example, there was a nine-month period when, due to financial issues, I didn't have a permanent home or a bed of my own. I either slept on the massage table, at an Airbnb, at various hotels, or in my car (which itself lasted over five months). I finally settled into my own safe place, only to have the anxiety rear its ugly head again three months later. That was because, again, I had seriously taxed my adrenal glands during that long, stressful experience—once I got into a place of safety and was no longer in a constant survival mode, they rebelled.

I came across an adrenal support supplement that I started taking, as well as an herb called Astragalus (which helps our bodies adapt to change). I took the adrenal support for six months before I noticed a difference. But I already knew that anything hormonal-related takes a good six to twelve months to see big improvement, if any. I didn't expect a quick fix, but I was confident that I needed to rebuild and support my adrenal glands.

Just a sidebar to the adrenals: There is a connection between the thyroid and your adrenal glands. Most people tend focus only on the thyroid. Because the thyroid is located in the throat, it is energetically related to your voice, expression of self, and speaking your truth. So, it makes sense that if your voice is shut off, your thyroid might physically shut off, as well. But in addition, your adrenal glands immediately sense danger, fear, and malfunction. Can you start to see the connection between the body, mind, and energy?

You have adrenal reflexes in your hands and feet, such that, if you rub them, you can help stimulate your adrenal glands. Personally, I practice stimulating my adrenals, via the adrenal reflexes, each morning. This is the foundation behind Reflexology—the concept that our bodies have reflexes (pressure points) along the bottoms of the feet and palms of the hands, correlating to other areas of the body. Therefore, if you stimulate (massage, rub) those reflex points, it will help to stimulate the same corresponding area of your body. For example, rubbing the sinus points in your feet can possibly help your sinuses.

Vegetable Juice

You cannot go wrong with vegetable juice. Vegetable juicing is greatly nourishing for the whole body and is, energetically, high vibrational. Right now, every cell in your body desires large amounts of love. Love energy enables your insides to run well and feel brighter. Vegetable juice is produced when the juicer removes the insoluble fiber so that only the nutrients and soluble fiber remain—this is where the antioxidants are. Because the insoluble fiber has been removed, your body uses the juice very quickly, so I like to call vegetable juice "quick nutrition in a glass." Prior to my anxiety issues, I was already a regular juicer. So, I amped up the amount I was drinking, and it always made me feel good.

You can make vegetable juice yourself or go to a local juice bar. There are a range of vegetable juices out there, but the darker green ones will be more nourishing for you during your healing process. When you first learn to juice, it's best to keep your juice simple. The best fruits and vegetables to juice include lettuces, carrots, celery, apples, cucumbers, grapefruit (rind off), lemons (always organic, because you keep the peel on), and beets (never more than golf ball sized). You can do any combination of these. A good beginner's juice consists of lettuce, carrots, and apples. Be sure to sip and chew your juice, as that unlocks the flavor and helps your body digest it faster. Do not add ice to your juice. Ice greatly delays the digestion of the juice, because your body has to warm it up first before it can utilize the nutrients, which is the opposite of what you want—quick nutrition for the body.

The cookbook I was working on—put on the back burner (pun intended) in order to write this book— focuses on vegetable juices and smoothies. So, if that's your jam, keep following me.

Liver Cleanses

Liver cleansing also fits nicely in this section, because it is a profound experience for any type of healing journey or simply for a healthy life, in general. Your liver is like the oil filter for your body. Just like your car, your liver needs to be cleansed out every spring and fall. Your liver has over four hundred known functions and literally plays a role in every aspect of your health! It's a very pivotal organ. Your liver holds on to all kinds of toxins, both physical (ie, medications, low vibrational foods, liver stones, or gallstones) and emotional (like hurt, anger, trauma, unforgiveness, or jealousy). So, if you've already undergone a lot of healing, whether physical or emotional, doing a liver cleanse can be the last step to help push the toxins out of your physical being.

I have done around eighty liver cleanses, and the results are always different. No matter why I do a liver cleanse, though, I always have another layer of healing fall away.

There are two types of liver cleanses. The first is a "scratch the surface" kind, where you drink some teas, pop some pills, and take some fiber for three days to a week. The other is what I call the "down and dirty" version. This version is where you commit to getting your liver and colon ready for six weeks prior to the cleanse, through the use of enemas and/or colonics, vegetable juicing, lymphatic drainage massage, drinking dandelion tea, eating an elimination diet, and so forth. It's not for the faint of heart, but rather, for those who deeply desire to eliminate toxins, who can commit, and who can follow detailed directions. Because the step-by-step instructions are their own guide, I'm not going to include the liver cleanse here;

however, you can access the guide through the Resources section of the book.

Enemas and Colonics

One of my disciplines is in Colon Hydro-Therapy—that makes me a colon hydro-therapist (CHT). Enemas help to remove the cycle and recirculation of toxins that can further irritate the body, which can also compound anxiety. Nothing good comes from trash (poop) sitting at 98.6 degrees, especially if it's stockpiling (constipation). Toxins from the bowels will reenter the bloodstream if they aren't leaving the body fast enough or they end up in areas that aren't designed to house those kinds of toxins.

Enemas are like brushing your teeth, except that it happens in your intestines; it's like sweeping a broom along your colon wall. Our bodies are made up of mostly water, which is why washing our insides out with water works so well—it is super hydrating and cleans out unhealthy toxins. Water is one of the best ways to clear and shift the body's energy and is particularly profound when done *inside* of the body. The first time you do a colonic or enema may seem weird, but everyone usually talks about how much lighter they feel inside after doing them.

See the Resources section to find out more about enemas and colonics.

Miscellaneous Therapies

Here are a couple of other therapies I tried along my healing journey.

O2 bar: I'm not sure how much it actually helped, but at the time, I figured that it couldn't hurt to increase my oxygen levels. I remember the O2 bar was over an hour drive away, which could have been anxiety-inducing, but I was so determined to find something...anything that would do the trick and resolve my anxiety, that I was willing to take the chance. I was desperate to find the thing, or combination of things, that would work for me.

Quantum biofeedback: This process helps to shift the energy vibrations that correspond to everything in your body. Biofeedback is all about working with frequencies that can cause stress on the body. Stress constricts everything, especially the energy flow in the body and organs. Emotions, foods, chemicals, and heavy metals are just some of the things that can cause stress, resulting in blockages in the internal organs and glands. The physical blockages can, then, cause energetic blockages to occur, leading to inflammation and health issues. Biofeedback focuses on all points of stress. This technique was one I practiced for quite a while, at different times along my journey. Even though I only saw incremental improvement with biofeedback, I believed it was helping me in a way I didn't yet understand.

Self-Reflection

1. How does anxiety show up physically for you? It's helpful to identify it and write it out. Get really detailed. It's helpful to dissect anxiety to remove its power over you. It can be hard to look at it at first, but it's worth it in the long run.
2. Do you identify with the Adrenal fatigue symptoms?
3. Do you live in a "fight or flight" state? If so, why?
4. Do you feel unsafe?

CONDITIONS THAT MIMIC

I dentifying and separating out the conditions that mimic anxiety can help lessen the power of anxiety over you. Similar to a virus or parasite that hides itself in the host body, mimicking other conditions, you often don't recognize the real culprit. Once you identify what *isn't* anxiety, you are able to see the real version more clearly and hopefully, realize that it's not anything to be afraid of.

Epstein-Barr Virus

Epstein-Barr virus is what causes Mononucleosis (Mono). However, you can have the virus without ever having the full-blown version of Mono. It's called the "kissing virus" because you can easily get it from kissing (saliva). Many people have it without realizing they do —if you have ever kissed even one person, you could have contracted the virus. When I first contracted it, I had swollen lymph nodes in my neck for weeks, had no energy, and felt general malaise. I did everything I knew, holistically, to support my lymph nodes and boost my immunity—garlic, massaging my lymph nodes, Epsom salt soaks, enemas, rosemary essential oil on my lymph nodes, and more. I pieced together the symptoms to figure out what was going on. Over the years, following that initial bout, I would have dormant stages interspersed with active stages, experiencing symptoms, such as fever, rapid heart rate, anxiety and chills.

It's interesting that, for me, the virus had an emotional component, as well, which I realized was related to the narcissism I had experienced in my early years. The more I worked on myself and forgave, the less and less the virus would bother me. A virus is just like a parasite. It mimics the body or some other condition, so that you don't know it is there, hiding in the body while it wreaks havoc. During the active stages, the virus would usually manifest in me feeling overwhelmed by anxious thoughts, followed by chills, then flushes of warmth. I would spike a fever and my heart would pound. The anxious thoughts would disappear once the chills set in and then I would spike the fever, at which point I would heave a sigh of relief because I recognized what was happening—it was a viral attack, not a panic attack. Usually the whole course, from beginning to end (onset of anxiety to the fever subsiding) would last only a couple of hours. The intensity of it could range from being mild to severe, where I would feel extremely drained afterwards.

As in my case, there can be both a physical component to the Epstein-Barr virus (and a test to determine if you have it) but also an underlying emotional tie. Again, this is why it's important to notice all aspects of the anxiety. Are the symptoms always the same or does the anxiety manifest in various ways? At the slightest symptom, the tendency can be to immediately lump it all together into one explanation. For example, I have noticed that being cold and having my neck bare causes my body temperature to drop. As a result, my body will then spike a fever to get my temperature up, and that can cause a short viral attack.

One way to detect a fever when you're feeling anxious is to put your wrists on your forehead and notice if your forehead feels a little warm. You can also ask yourself if your lower back or forearms are achy? Pay attention to any other symptoms you usually get when you have a fever.

Boost your immune system via herbs, relaxation, Lymphatic Drainage massage, glandular support, Epsom salt soaks, and chlorophyll. B vitamins support your nervous system, as well. Rosemary, oregano, and L-Lysine can help kill viruses, too. When your immune system is rocky, any type of change in the body, such as hormones or inflammation, can depress the immune system and spike an illness.

Anemia

There are different types of anemia; however, in general, anemia is a reduced number of healthy red blood cells. Because red blood cells carry oxygen, if you have anemia, you will have a lack of oxygen in the blood. One way to tell if you are anemic is to pull down your eyelid and take note of the color of the inside of your eyelid. A nice pink color is a good indicator of oxygen in your body. Pale pink or white indicates that your oxygen levels are low.

Menstruating women bleed every month, and yet, we often do nothing to encourage rebuilding every month. Yes, our body is supposed to do that automatically, but what if we purposely helped it to rebuild?

Your lymphatic system plays a role in your red blood cell count in that, if the lymphatic system drips fat into your bloodstream too fast, it kills red blood cells. So, it's important for your lymphatic system to be working properly, as well.

One way to address anemia is by taking one tablespoon of liquid chlorophyll in eight ounces of water, one tablespoon of blackstrap molasses, and vitamin E (based on your weight), daily until better. vitamin E and vitamin C are helpful to take together, as they each complement the other. vitamin E is a fat-soluble vitamin, so it works better when taken with other fats during a meal. Additionally, there are excellent blood-cleansing teas out there that can support the health of your blood and whole body, such as red clover, sheep sorrel, and violet leaf. These are also available in herbal tincture form.

TMJ and Fascia

One day on the way to work, I was feeling a little anxious and started rubbing my jaw (the temporo-mandibular joint, or TMJ, area). As I did, I felt a literal *shutting off* of my breathing; a tightness wrapped itself around my throat. In that moment, I realized that tight jaws or jaw clenching can also feel like anxiety—it's yet another symptom that can mimic it.

TMJ dysfunction can wrap tension around your throat and suppress your breathing. It can even trigger fascial strain that runs down to the ribcage and wraps around your chest. Fascial strain is strain of the fascia. Think of the TMJ as the hub of a wheel—any tension or strain can pull forward into the face, up to the top of your head, to the back of your head, or down into your shoulders. If your jaw is tight, your lower back is probably also tight, as are your calves, ankles, and feet. The fascial pattern (tension strain) will pull from the top to the bottom of your body. Fascial strain plays a role in TMJ dysfunction.

Fascia runs throughout your entire body, like an inner webbing that holds your muscles together, providing structure and support. The IT (iliotibial) band on the side of your leg is fascia, all your ligaments are fascia, and part of your tendons are, too. If you were to cut a piece of meat in half and see the silvery stuff, that is fascia. If it's tight, it holds your muscles tight, restricts blood and lymph flow, restricts nerve conduction, and pulls on bone structures. It can pull up to two thousand pounds per square inch and can land you in the emergency room for unexplained pain. The hospital then gives you muscle relaxers and sends you home. Although this works, by relaxing the body tissue, it doesn't correct the issue.

The fascia also holds on to ALL emotional and physical trauma, from whiplash, to sneezing, to birth strain, to your parents' divorce—everything spanning from in-utero to the present day. It is constantly trying to unwind its tension and trauma. This is why babies fuss, and move around, and stretch, and why kids often cry for "no apparent reason." As the years go by, we are told to *hold still, don't look weird*, causing us to tune out what our body is trying to tell us.

What do you know about your own birth? How you arrived in the world and what you experienced in the womb greatly impacts your being. Were you a happily received pregnancy? Was your mom stressed while carrying you? Or, were you an unwanted birth? How was your birth? Do you know the details about your birth? These are questions most people don't think to ask, but we need to ask! How you came into this world is very important. If you are adopted, do you know anything about your birth parents and their situation? You would pick up on their situation in the womb. You might even have a *knowing* about yourself or a conditioning that you can't explain. Any broken bones, surgeries, dental work, parents' divorce, stress, hormones, your own heartbreak or divorce, children/birth, miscarriages...your body holds on to ALL of this and buries it physically and emotionally into your fascia, if it is not allowed to process out in a healthy manner.

The Gillespie Approach is a next-level therapy that works by unwinding the fascia layers. The Gillespie Approach helps to peel back the layers of memory or injury or whatever is preventing you from healing at a deeper level. Working with the fascia is both physically and emotionally (if you allow it to be) therapeutic. It unwinds the "trauma onion" layer by layer, according to what layer it deems most important to let go of, which may or may not match what *you* perceive to be most important. Whenever I've had it done, I'd cry afterwards—a sign of relief and release. I've even had clients switch from massage to The Gillespie Approach or combine it with massage because it works wonders! Find out more about The Gillespie Approach in the Resources section of the book.

The sternocleidomastoid muscles (SCM) are responsible for turning your head, as well as raising your ribcage when breathing. They run from behind your ear, down your neck, and attach to your collarbone. They often become overworked with smoking, coughing, and asthma. If tight, they can contribute to TMJ dysfunction and reduced movement of the ribcage.

It is suggested that you find a therapist that does The Gillespie Approach to really get to the underlying cause. Meanwhile, something you can do at home is work on your TMJs by massaging your jaws and temples. You can also take a clean finger, slide it along your gums to the back "joint" and massage there. It is also beneficial to massage under your tongue—hook your finger under your tongue, slide it to the side, under the jaw bone, and massage back and forth. This spot might be tender, but it's one of your Pterygoid muscles that helps make up the TMJ. You can do this after brushing your teeth, first thing in the morning, or even while you sit at a red light.

Chewing gum will annoy and overwork the TMJs. Chewing gum can be a distraction when you suffer from anxiety or nervousness; it may also be that you unconsciously know that you have tension there and need some relief. Massaging your TMJs can help eliminate the need to have chewing gum. There have been times after receiving The Gillespie Approach technique that my jaws felt so relaxed that I couldn't keep my mouth closed afterward! It was awesome!

Another issue that can negatively affect your TMJs is parasites. Grinding your teeth and jaws at night can be a sign of parasites in your body. And yes, everyone has parasites. It's part of your microbiome to have a balance of good and bad bacteria in your body. However, when it's out of balance, it becomes a problem, and one sign is teeth grinding. Parasite cleansing is a unique therapy and should be done with caution, in conjunction with enemas or colonics, so their dead bodies leave as soon as they die. Fresh, raw garlic is beneficial for killing parasites and is also excellent for cholesterol control, and as an anti-bacterial, anti-viral, and anti-fungal (not to mention keeping toxic people away)! Garlic took on the nickname of Russian penicillin when it was discovered, during both world wars, to be anti-septic after they ran out of their regular medicine. You can consume it raw by itself, but it might feel uncomfortable in your stomach. Adding fresh garlic to guacamole, butter, salsa, pesto, or as a last-minute sprinkle to any of your cooked dishes as you plate, are all excellent ways to get more of this anti-parasitic wonder food into your body.

Low Body Temperature

At one point, I started to notice a cycle in which, if my neck was cold, in addition to my upper back, or ankles and calves, my body would spike a temperature. I would feel like I had a fever so that my body would get me warm again. How does a person feel with a fever? Achy, tired, anxious, chilled, heart pounding, and flushes of warmth. I noticed that the symptoms would range from a very mild case to a full-on fever.

A lower body temperature, or not being able to handle air conditioning (I barely like the AC on), can spike a fever. Did you know that women's limbs are 2.5 degrees lower in temperature than men? That's why women are often colder than men. However, a woman's core must remain warm enough to carry and grow babies. The feminine energy is cool, the masculine energy is warm. My own baseline temperature is 97.5 degrees, which is lower than the "average" body. I've discovered over the years what areas of my body must be covered for me to feel warm...typically, my feet, upper back, and neck.

A funny situation occurred during 2020, when we were required to have our temperature taken upon entering a building. I went to dinner with some co-workers, and at the restaurant, no one was manning the thermometer. Everyone did it themselves, which was a moot point. But when I took my temperature, it was 96.5! I chuckled to myself and thought, "Well, apparently I'm dead and no one cares!" But think about it, if everyone has a different temperature, a person could have a fever at the "normal" 98.6 degrees. Therefore, knowing your baseline is important!

A low body temperature could also be a sign of your thyroid being unhappy, since your thyroid is responsible for body temperature. Your adrenal glands play a slight role in temperature, as well. If your body is stressed out by being too cold or too hot, the adrenals work overtime to keep your insides at homeostasis. As an aside, vitamin C can also help your body handle extreme temperatures.

One of the ways you can figure out your baseline temperature is to take your temperature for one week, every morning before you get out of bed, and then average it out. When I did it, years ago, I put the thermometer under my tongue, but I've seen information recently stating that under the armpit is more accurate. Research it yourself, and find out what works best for you.

Self-Reflection

1. Ask about your birth: Were you a happily received pregnancy? Or, were you an unwanted birth? How was your birth? Do you know the details of your birth? These are questions most people don't think to ask—ask! How you came into this world is very important. If you are adopted, do you know anything about your birth parents and their situation?
2. Do you spike a fever with your anxiety? Check your forehead against the underside of your wrist. Does your forehead feel warm when you have anxiety? Do you also have a fever headache (top of head)? Are there any other achy fever sites like lower back, knees, or forearms that occur at the same time?
3. Do your jaws ache? Do you grit your teeth or get tension headaches?
4. Does Epstein-Barr Virus sound like a factor to you?

4

RELAXATION IS THE NAME OF
THE GAME

R elaxation is the name of the game. Period. Relaxation is huge to help rest, reset, and repair your adrenal glands and stop the anxiety cycle. But relaxation may be hard at first, because your mind is all over the place, and it freaks out about holding still and feeling "trapped." Afterwards, though, you are so relaxed that it's worth it! You'll find yourself looking forward to it more and more. In this chapter, I share my top relaxation methods.

Sleep

Sleep is essential because it helps you to relax, think more clearly, and restore your adrenal glands. It is important to view your bedroom as a sanctuary, a sacred place to sleep. If your bedroom is a collection spot for overflow from the rest of the house, then it will feel cluttered and unclean, rather than soothing or relaxing.

I have received tons of client compliments over the years, folks who said that they wished their bedroom looked and felt as comforting as my massage room. With that in mind, here are some tips on how to create a sleep haven...the essential place to relax, sleep, and have sex.

- Keep your bedroom simple and clean.
- Place an amazing comforter on your bed, one that feels good on your skin. If you are cold-natured, be sure the comforter is heavy enough to keep you warm.
- Keep your sheets fresh.
- Remove everything from your bedroom that is unrelated to bedroom activity.
- Clean the floors and add a comfortable, decorative rug for your feet.
- Consider adding a salt lamp and/or a few flameless (or real) candles.
- Utilize soft lighting, a sound machine, and/or a device that plays music, if desired.

- Keep the room warm, comfortable, and inviting.
- Add beautiful and easy-to-care-for plants, such as a snake plant, peace lily, or pothos, to encourage better air quality and give the space a homey vibe.
- Consider purchasing an air purifier.

Sometimes, people have difficulty falling asleep. One common reason is taking a multivitamin too late in the day, often because you don't want to take them in the morning on an empty stomach, which can cause stomach upset. In general, multivitamins are designed to be taken in the morning, and that is because the B vitamins in them provide an energy boost. As an aside, an upset stomach in the morning can also be caused by constipation, when the peristaltic wave tries to move things through; if the wave hits a roadblock, it can feel yucky or crampy. When this happens, you may also notice that you still feel full from the night before. From a Colon Hydro-therapist's viewpoint, a yucky belly in the morning is not something to be ignored, long-term; it is essentially your gut asking for help.

Teas like chamomile can assist with sleep, as can certain herbal tinctures. But always remember, when using herbal tinctures, be mindful of possible medication interactions. If your intention is to slowly wean yourself off of a medication, then do so wisely and under the supervision of your doctor. Essential oils that support sleep include lavender, frankincense, vetiver, and wild orange. You can diffuse them, add them to your bath, or rub them into the bottoms of your feet.

When I was on the anxiety rollercoaster, I couldn't wait for bedtime, because I knew that I would get a reprieve from the mind overwhelm.

Exercise

Exercise provides an excellent hormone boost. It helps to shift your mindset and shed the stress that can pull down your adrenal glands. It helps you stay fit and increases your appetite. I encourage you to find some type of exercise that you enjoy, whether it be dancing, yoga, Pilates, or full on beast mode. But it doesn't necessarily have to look like your typical form of exercise, if you can't stand that approach. Exercise promotes a healthy body and mind. As you progress, trust yourself to know when it's time for a new way of movement or longer or shorter sessions. Don't judge yourself on this one—let it be your own journey.

I remember when I was struggling a little with sleeping, and my anxiety was at an all-time high, it was suggested that I start exercising, because that would help me decrease stress, increase sleep, provide me with feel-good oxytocin, and give my adrenal glands a break. So, I started to do some workouts and immediately suffered from sore muscles. I was advised to keep working out, that it would be worth it. And, it was! I currently enjoy a combination of Pilates, strength training, and dancing.

Another benefit of exercise it that it helps to establish a healthy "heart pounding" vs anxiety "heart pounding." As you experience a good heart pounding from working out, then the other is less likely to scare you.

Massage

An hour-long massage session helps to reset your body, soothe your nervous system, and is equivalent to eight hours of sleep. Physical touch grounds you, taking you out of your head and placing you back into your body. It also combats stress-related high blood pressure, reduces headaches, and keeps you limber, providing protection from injury. Massage soothes the nervous system, through the actual massage strokes, as well as the overall sensation of touch. It helps you to relax...to be quiet and still. It will also loosen any tight muscles. Frequent massage will remind your body what "good" feels like.

Of course, being a massage therapist, I recommend this particular modality wholeheartedly! I can always tell when a person who comes in for a massage is anxious; I pick up on those cues quite easily. One obvious sign is that the client will talk nonstop, because they are so uncomfortable being quiet.

Give yourself four weekly massage sessions in a row and notice how you feel in your body and mind. It's an excellent stress management tool.

Epsom Salt Soaks

I swear by Epsom salt soaks, in no small part because they have kept me going as a massage therapist. Salt baths soothe my muscles and often help to shift my mindset. For me, it's twenty minutes of mandatory self-care and stillness. I've also noticed that salt baths help to clear the energy field around me after working on people all day.

Epsom salt is full of magnesium, which relaxes the muscles, as well as the mind. It's also detoxing for the skin and lymphatic system. And a nice, salt bath will warm you up, if you tend to be cold. Salt baths are a wonderful sleep aid, since they soothe your muscles, clear your aura, ground you, and drop you into your body. All of this helps you to be still, which is very important. You can make this process as fun and creative as you want to! For example, you could add candles, soft music, a good book, essential oils (lavender or frankincense), and/or some herbs (chamomile, lavender flowers, skullcap, passionflower). You could even place some cut flowers in the bathroom. Make the soak a special time of sacred self-care.

As a reminder, do not use synthetic bubble bath, as it will affect the pH of the vaginal area. To be honest, bubble baths don't mix well with Epsom salts.

To create an Epsom salt soak, put two cups of Epsom salt in a tub full of pleasantly warm to hot water (depending on your preference). Step in and soak for twenty minutes. It can be beneficial to sip on some water while soaking. Drain the bathwater and then briefly rinse off afterwards to remove any toxins that might have been released.

Relaxing Music

Clients over the years have marveled about how relaxing the music is that I have played in the massage room. It is so easy to find and start using! One idea is to start playing soothing music about an hour before bedtime. If you have kids, you might notice that it helps them to chill out, as well. When you find some good, relaxing music, take a moment to read the comments. You'll notice that you most certainly aren't the only one seeking relief for your soul. In my teens and twenties, I listened to anything BUT relaxing music. Now, I greatly treasure it and am even listening as I write this book!

Get Outside

Outside...sunshine...warmth! As little as fifteen minutes a day of fresh air and sunlight is beneficial. Being in the sunshine is my happy place; it warms me up, uplifts my spirit, grounds me, and relaxes me. I prefer to have the sun shining directly on me, particularly on my forehead (the location of my third eye) and into my pineal gland (which is responsive to light and sound). Since I was a teenager, I have found solace in the sunshine. I instinctively knew that, no matter what was happening, if I could just spend some time in the sun, I'd feel better. If my stomach felt yucky or I had period cramps, for example, going outside was rejuvenating. Even if I was stuck inside working, just being able to see the sunshine through a window would make me smile and be grateful.

Technology might be advanced, but we are still human creatures who need elements of the outdoors to feel calm within. What's more, walking outside can become a moving meditation.

Intentional Tension Release

I didn't realize how tense I was growing up; I was always so on-guard. Tension over a long period of time is what wears down the adrenal glands. When you are being attacked, even in the most subtle, mind-controlled ways, you don't realize how tense you are until you aren't anymore.

Find ways to relax your jaw, your calves, and your feet —there seems to be a strain pattern that pulls from the top of the head down the back to the feet. More people need to learn how to massage themselves. For example, just sit down and start massaging your feet. Some people are so out of tune with their own bodies that even touching themselves in a loving way makes them afraid of looking weird. So, they reserve it just for the massage therapist. Please work on your own body...

touch your body, know your body, and talk to your body...tell your body it's ok. Finding ways to release tension is important, because when you start to relax, you begin to realize just how tense you were.

Rocking

Just as a baby is soothed when rocked or bounced, rocking our adult bodies is just as important, because whether with babies or adults, it helps to soothe the nervous system. Rocking can be as simple as sitting in a rocker, a hammock, or a swing. Another form of rocking we might do as humans is when we are standing and we start to sway our bodies. In a way, that's also rocking ourselves.

I discovered with The Gillespie Approach (craniosacral fascial therapy) clients that sometimes during the session, their legs would want to be rocked. That's when I made the connection—rocking of the legs, rocking in a rocking chair, rocking in a hammock or swing—the simple act of rocking calms and regulates the nervous system, if needed. I had clients who loved the rocking of their legs so much that if a session ended without their legs rocking (which was actual progress) they would be upset.

Magnesium

Most people are deficient in Magnesium. In massage school we learned that your body required two minerals to help your muscles function: calcium, to retract (tighten) your muscles and magnesium, to relax your muscles. Calcium is promoted across the board. Magnesium is not. Magnesium is also a natural statin (there goes the whole cholesterol business). It is an excellent remedy for cramps, headaches, sleeping, and more. If you take synthetic magnesium, too much will give you diarrhea. However, if you take a high quality, absorbable form, you won't have that issue. Another consideration is that magnesium needs to be taken in balance with calcium or it won't work well.

You should be able to tell within a couple of months if the magnesium is working, because the headaches, sleeping difficulty, and cramps should be noticeably better. That being said, with regard to menstrual cramps, it is only fair to give it two to four months to work, so that both ovaries have a couple of cycles to go through with the new support of magnesium. There are several different ways to take magnesium: on the skin application, liquid, capsules and powder. Epsom salt baths are full of magnesium, too. The skin soaks it up during a salt bath, which is why you feel so relaxed afterwards. However, don't ever ingest Epson salt, as it'll give you massive diarrhea.

In summary, I can't stress enough how critical relaxation is in the management of anxiety. As a testament to its importance, I realized that I had written about the significance of relaxation five different times during my initial brain dump prior to writing this book! SOOO it's VERY valuable!

Self-Reflection

1. When was the last time you truly felt relaxed?
2. What prevents you from prioritizing relaxation?
3. Go look at your bedroom—does it invite sleep? Is it noisy with electronics?
4. How can you schedule in some self-care, no matter your budget?
5. What relaxation methods are you most drawn to?
6. What is one thing from the relaxation techniques in this chapter that you haven't yet tried but you will start incorporating into your routine?

OTHER PIECES OF THE PUZZLE

As I mentioned before, anxiety is multi-faceted. So, it is helpful to separate anxiety from other types of tightness or restriction within your body. In this chapter, I share a few more pieces of the puzzle— issues that could contribute to an unhappy body, as well as other helpful suggestions and ideas to consider as you focus on your healing.

Bras

I could go down a whole tangent about how bras are not healthy. First of all, we wear them because we are conditioned to by our mom, society, and religion. BUT NONE OF THE REASONS GIVEN ARE ACTUALLY FOR OUR HEALTH! The only time a bra is truly helpful is when the boobs need some support—during breast-feeding, for heavy chested women, or for protection. A tight bra is like a corset around your ribcage. Most women put off purchasing a properly fitted bra or are afraid of not wearing one. But, a tight bra will restrict the diaphragm from taking in a full breath, causing shallow breathing. Another consideration is that tight bra straps or sports bras can cut into the shoulder muscles (upper traps), leading to even tighter shoulders, a tight neck, or TMJ tension! I believe a good number of chiropractors would agree that most women are subluxated (meaning, there is a slight misalignment of the vertebrae) at the bra line.

Because I am trained in lymphatic drainage massage, I also understand that bras, in general, will slow down your lymphatic system, which is a big NO with regard to breast health. It seems that women traded corsets for bras and unfortunately, aren't any better off.

Remember, your boobs are beautiful and heart centered.

So, how can we make the best decision with regard to wearing a bra? I believe that every woman must listen to their own inner guidance on this issue and, just as important, DO NOT JUDGE what others choose to do.

Teas*

I have found that drinking relaxing teas are soothing, grounding, warming, and can assist in creating a relaxation routine. Most of the herbal teas I have consumed are mild tasting. If herbal teas scare you, just add some raw honey.

Herbal teas consist of dried flowers, leaves, stems, roots, bark, seeds, or berries. Just like spices, herbs in the dried form are more concentrated than fresh herbs or spices. Trust what you are drawn to make, tea-wise; however, you might consider chamomile (but not if you have ragweed allergies), skullcap, passionflower, lemon balm, oat straw, or catnip.

To make an herbal tea, start by putting a tea bag or a heaping teaspoon of loose-leaf tea into your mug. Then, pour eight ounces of boiling water over it, and cover it with a small plate or saucer for fifteen minutes. This is called *steeping* the tea, so that it doesn't let any of the "goods" escape via steam. Once it has steeped long enough, take off the lid, and let it cool to your preferred tea temperature before drinking. At this point, you may add a teaspoon of honey, if desired. Sometimes, you will notice a difference right away; other times, you might want to drink a particular tea for a few nights in a row to see if you feel any benefit. (As an aside, heating up water in the microwave is not the same as boiling water.)

Constipation

Having a yucky GI tract and slow bowels can really pull a body down! Nothing good happens when trash sits at 98.6 degrees, particularly for long periods of time. Your bowels, being a part of your gut, are understood in the holistic realm as the "second brain," so what happens in that area (toxins, slow bowels, inflammation) can affect the clarity of mind or create a foggy brain. Thus, having slow bowels can have a compound effect on an already unhealthy situation. Constipation can also cause irregular periods and low back pain and contribute to yeast infections and bad breath. Lastly, constipation could potentially impact fertility.

Having healthy bowel movements—technically three times a day—is critical. After every meal, you should move your bowels, because the chewing motion of the mouth muscles starts the peristaltic wave. This motion runs through the whole digestive tract, from the mouth to the anus. This wave transports nourishment through the GI tract. So, when food is brought into the body, waste should leave the body.

Things that can positively impact the bowels include relaxation, chia seeds, flax seeds (ground up), an apple a day, a chiropractic visit, enemas, and/or colonics. Massaging your belly first thing in the morning is also helpful. Massage from your right hip, then up under your right rib cage, straight across to just under your left rib cage, down to your left hip, and then across to under your belly button. Then, gently press down three times, in a clock-wise motion. At first, you might not notice anything. Nevertheless, keep at it, as this process helps to re-tone your bowel.

Sexual Pleasure

Sexual pleasure changes your energy. Introducing energy orgasms. Don't skip over this one. Sexual pleasure, whether penis or vagina/clitoris stimulation, helps to release "feel good" hormones...and very powerful ones, too. I was beginning to learn about energy orgasms when 2020 hit. I would go to the grocery store and the energy was SOOO heavy and unbearable. I came up with a method to counteract those negative energies. While standing in line to check out my groceries, I would breathe deeply into my private area; it would immediately spasm, and I would feel an energy orgasm run through my body. My lower stomach would tighten, and I could feel it coming up through my body (my chakras), sometimes stronger than others. I've done it multiple times to help shift me out of negative energy. Nothing is stronger or feels more ecstatic than an orgasm, and you can stay in that effect, mind-wise, for quite a while.

Sexy daydreaming can also help take you out of a negative space, as well, (or frankly, whatever you'd truly prefer to think about instead of your anxiety). Granted, if you are super anxious, then even sex can make you feel panicked, rather than inducing an enjoyable experience. If that is the case, perhaps an energy orgasm is a better alternative for you at that time. Again, it's important to separate true anxiety from healthy heart pounding.

Here is a method of practice: If you are used to yoga, then you understand how your instructor will encourage you to breathe deeply into any area of tightness, and you can feel your breath going into those areas. Breathe deeply into your genital area. You can either let it brew in that area or pull the energy up your body. Really focus on where you are feeling the energy; you may need to practice a few times to get the hang of it. Focused breathing, in general, is yet another way to break the anxiety pattern. You can practice it when you first get into bed.

I value feeling good so much that I purposefully do not participate in feeling bad! In other words, I *choose* to find and practice ways to feel good. When I was feeling overwhelmed with anxiety to the point where I was just tired of being stuck in it, then I would remind myself of what I've done before to help me out of it. I decided, instead, to choose the thoughts that I DO want to think about. When I was working with the Amish years ago, hating every minute of it, while also suffering from anxiety, I would fantasize about sex. Any thoughts about sex will, naturally, put you in a better "feel good" energy. When I had that breakthrough about feeling *on purpose*, I was determined to get better. I thought to myself, "Hell no! You are not stealing my time and energy any longer! I am not giving you any more control of my beautiful life."

Essential Oils*

Essential oils are leaves, flowers, bark, roots, or fruit that have been steam distilled—the steam that is collected becomes the essential oil, and the water that is left over is used for perfume. You can use essential oils in a diffuser, on your feet, or in your bathtub (depending on the brand and whether they are skin safe).

In all the years I had been in the natural health field, I was never interested in essential oils. Partly because I didn't understand what they were, and they often didn't smell pure. One day a fellow massage therapist, who also takes a holistic perspective, asked me to come to a class she was putting on. Since we tended to think alike, I went, without even asking what the class was about. Once I got there, I realized that the class was about essential oils. What grabbed my attention, however, was how pure and authentic the oils were. I understood, right then, what they were and how they worked. One suggestion that really caught my attention during that class was, if you combine lemongrass, white fir, and black pepper, it can help heal ligaments! As a massage therapist this was gold! From that point on, I have used essential oils, along with my teas and herbal tinctures as staples in my holistic toolkit.

There are several essential oils that work particularly well for those who are healing from anxiety. Lavender is calming and helps you fall asleep. While vetiver can knock a person out (sleep-wise), it smells like burnt tires and is thick like maple syrup, so I tend to only use that one on my feet. Citrus, interestingly, is both calming and energizing. Woodsy essential oils (like sandalwood and cedarwood) will help ground you. I really like putting sandalwood and bergamot together, as they are both uplifting and grounding at the same time. At one point on my anxiety journey, I would use lavender and Chill Out herbal tincture (one that I make) almost every hour to keep me calm. Check out the Resources section for more recommended essential oils.

Herbal Tinctures*

Herbal tinctures are created by taking herbs (fresh or dried leaves, fruit, berries, bark, roots, flowers) and covering them with either vodka, glycerin, or vinegar to draw out the medicinal components. They are, then, put in a dark cabinet and shaken every day for six weeks. After that, they are strained and either consumed straight (no dilution) or mixed with a bit of water or glycerin. Herbal tinctures are taken sublingually (under the tongue) where they enter the bloodstream immediately, allowing the body to use them accordingly. If the tincture is made with vodka, the body delivers it directly to the liver in order to utilize the herbal content.

The difference between supplements and herbs are that supplements, for the most part, support and nourish the body, while herbs tell your body what to do and how to function. So, both are necessary for healthy bodily function. I use supplements, essential oils, herbal teas, and herbal tinctures every day. They all have their place. However, I've learned to use my intuition to know what to take and when.

A link to some of the herbal tinctures I make in my apothecary can be found in the Resources section.

Note: Allergic reactions can occur with organic herbs. If you are pregnant or breastfeeding, make sure any herb is not contraindicated. Speak with a medical professional if you have any concerns or adverse reactions.

Hormones

We've already covered adrenal glands, which produce hormones, but there is a bit more to understand. Hormones are messengers—they instruct the different parts of your body. Did you know, for example, that certain hormones tell your heart to work faster or slower? Hormones, being high energy areas, will easily attract and hold on to heavy metals or toxins in your body. A healthy lifestyle can help keep toxins at a minimum. Everyone has hormones, and you want them to work well no matter your age. How do you support your hormones? Honestly, a healthy lifestyle is the best course of action.

It befuddles me that so many teenage girls are put on medication in their teens instead of being educated about the role of hormones. For example, it takes six years for your period and hormones to regulate after beginning to menstruate. During that timeframe, a teenager should be learning how to listen to their body, tracking their cycle, and understanding what the different fluids mean. They should be taught what herbs and hormone supports are most useful during different times of their cycle. I know plenty of women who have gone through a good portion of their lives depressed, simply because their hormones were out of balance! Once they got on hormone support, they felt much better.

Remember, when it comes to hormones, you have to give them about six to twelve months to see an improvement. So, stick with it. As mentioned earlier, a good adrenal support is incredibly helpful. I probably took one throughout my entire healing journey, until I felt like my anxiety was pretty much gone. Then, I would start it again if I became stressed, to give myself extra support during that time. If you are a woman, red raspberry tea is a great, all-around hormone health support to start. Saw Palmetto is wonderful for men, especially those over forty years of age. There is a plethora of herbs and herbal tinctures available that work to keep the hormones in balance. I make several of them under the guidance of a naturopathic doctor and herbalist. You can find information about them in the Resources section.

Lastly, it's important to discuss hormone support during pregnancy and nursing. I find it so ironic that, at the most important time of your life, hormone education is almost NEVER talked about. So many postpartum women suffer from extreme anxiety due to the variety of changes happening on all levels in their bodies. Plus, if you are breastfeeding, it will actually take more energy to grow your baby outside the womb than inside it. Again, hormone support is critical! This could take the form of a specialized herbal tincture (but not sage, as that will dry up your milk like nobody's business), having the placenta encapsulated to consume, or simply continuing your multivitamin after birth.

Alcohol and Caffeine

There are plenty of people who knowingly acknowledge that caffeine makes them anxious and yet they keep drinking it! Caffeine is not my friend. The last time I had coffee I had heart palpitations for two hours afterwards. After that, I said, "Never again!" And I haven't had coffee since. I do love the smell of coffee though, so I get that with my body scrub, as coffee is a good lymph stimulant through the skin.

Caffeine can also be found in high quality, dark chocolate. So if you eat chocolate late in the day and have issues falling asleep, it could be the natural caffeine in the dark chocolate.

Same thing with alcohol. A lot of people say alcohol makes them feel anxious, as well. Anything that makes you feel poorly is letting your body know it is not good for it. Pain, exhaustion, extreme thirst...it's all feedback from your body, letting you know that something is not working, so please listen.

Food Sensitivity

If your body is already in an unhealthy state, whether that be your mindset or your physicality, then a food sensitivity, such as to gluten, dairy, corn, or sugar, for example, is just going to make you feel even more lousy. The food sensitivity could also be an underlying factor to your anxiety. For a lot of people, food fulfills a deep need for connection. Talking to people about food is like talking to them about religion and politics; they don't want to be told that they are wrong. They don't want to be told they need to change. They don't want to be told that what they're doing is not working for them.

I have helped thousands of people who have needed to make a switch, especially to a gluten-free lifestyle. It is not the end of the world if you decide to eliminate or alter a specific food item. If you do decide to go gluten-free, you need to give it at least six months, because that gives your body enough time to work the gluten toxins out.

How do you know if you have food sensitivities? You can get testing done and/or you can notice and log how you feel after eating certain foods. Do you feel nauseous? Do you feel overwhelmingly tired? Do you notice rashes or breakouts on your skin days later? Keeping a food journal is super helpful for this, and it's really not that much work. If you have time to check social media or stand in line, you have time to fill out a food journal. Keeping a journal (about anything) helps you to notice patterns over time.

B Vitamins and Your Nerves

Sugar and alcohol (which essentially turns into sugar in your body) strips your nervous system of B vitamins and other essential vitamins and minerals. B vitamins are what calm and nourish your nervous system. A teaspoon of sugar will kill thousands of white blood cells, and those are your immune cells! Sugar will lower your immunity, making you more susceptible to germs and illness. Sick season (winter) seems to correlate with lots of candy and sweets during the holiday season. If you love sweets, I encourage you to switch to a healthier version, such as maple syrup, coconut sugar, or honey. Once you start to lessen sugar from your diet, you'll notice your palette changing; sweets won't taste the same.

If you have an excessive craving for sweets, consider a parasite cleanse that is "wisely-guided," as parasites will make you crave sweets that you can't control. I say wisely-guided, because killing off parasites needs to be done in combination with colon cleansing and enemas, so that when you kill the parasites, they leave the body immediately and aren't re-infecting the body.

Sugar was never my friend. Even as a child, sugar was too much for my nervous system. People could tell if I had ingested sugar, because I would blink my eyes like crazy. Thankfully, I listened to my intuition; as a teenager and into adulthood, I have stayed away from it. Even now, if I eat sweets of the healthier version, I eat them towards the end of the day, in case they make me tired. I ate a regular gluten coffeecake once for break-fast, and I thought I was going to die from the gluten and the sugar; my system was in utter shock, not being used to any of that in the morning (or at all). It probably took me three hours to feel better. "Never again!" I thought. I learned my lesson.

So, if you compound a lagging nervous system with adrenal fatigue, plus tight muscles, your body is going to revolt. You may consider finding other ways to relax or socialize without alcohol. Or, develop the confidence to be able to socialize without drinking alcohol or having just water. You could also have water with lime and cranberry, so it looks like you're drinking, even if you're not.

How You Know You Are Healing

How can you know that you are healing and that all the work, effort, time, and money (and being your own best cheerleader) is working? One thing you'll notice is that you have an appetite! You might not even realize that you don't, but one day you notice HOW hungry you are. This applies to all healing in general—after having a baby, from grief, from surgery, from emotional stress or heartbreak. When you are feeling down or are pulled down by illness, your body isn't interested in eating...it even loses its appetite for life, for living.

When the desire to be free from religious abuse and narcissistic control was strong—when it was bigger than my fear of being anxious or being away from the house—that was my recognition that I WAS making progress. I was not attached. I was ready for my own freedom.

When your desire for change shows up for several days in a row, or you realize that you actually DO want to have some fun, or you want to try new things without a crutch...*that* moment makes you stop and realize that you HAVE come a long way, you have begun to heal... and *that* gives you more hope. You want something different from what you have been living. You are sick of what you have been doing. You want change. You've had enough.

Medication Side Effects

Since anxiety is usually multi-layered, medications may be impacting your anxiety. Are you on any medication that numbs out your true self? Take a look to see if anxiety is a side-effect of any of the medications that you are on. Then ask yourself, are you ok with that side effect? Is the reason for the medication more important than the anxiety you are experiencing while taking it? If not, you and your doctor may wish to develop a plan to wean yourself off the medication.

The Cycle of Stress, Immunity, and Hormones

As I listened to my body and started to see the repeating cycles of stress, I noticed that it would pull down my immune system and, during my monthly cycle, the hormones would spike the Epstein Barr Virus into action. You might start to notice your own cycle of stress and what spikes/activates the anxiety. What methods of prevention have you tried? For example, I would keep myself warm to prevent any virus attacks stemming from a low body temperature.

* THE INFORMATION SHARED in these sections is based on my own research, training in a multitude of disciplines, and personal experience with herbs. The information contained in this book should not be considered medical advice. These products are not intended to diagnose, treat, cure, or prevent any illness or disease. For diagnosis or treatment consult your physician.

Self-Reflection

1. Which one of the strategies or suggestions in this chapter stood out the most? How can you change or implement that piece?
2. What is your cycle of stress and anxiety? How can you change it?

PART II

EMOTIONAL/ENERGETIC

"A single blade of grass will push through cement seeking the light."

-Mary Morrisey

Keep in mind that with the healing journey, the last place for the energetic and emotional healing to leave is in the physical body. For example, there have been times where, after some healing, my period may seem different, but then normal the following month. Or maybe there is a new issue that appeared out of nowhere and is unexplainable. However, after looking back, it seems like it came along after some sort of healing process.

Stress is all emotional and energetic. Think about it, you cannot *see* stress. It's based on how you *feel*. Internalized stress leads to 99.9% of all illnesses and diseases. The more you can do to reduce your stress and relax (in a healthy way) the better you'll feel.

Let me re-share the dedication with you—what you are seeking is seeking you. Know that if what you are looking for—peace, calmness, groundedness, relaxation, clarity of mind, being able to consciously choose your thoughts—is also looking for you, you will find it. If you are reading this book, that means that you are in the process of overcoming your anxiety. In the moment of you desiring something better, that's the moment that change happens. You might not see it right away, but put forth the effort and you will.

Taking a multifaceted approach is best if you want to support yourself as much as possible, because it all adds up. It all helps, and it must work. Thus far, this book has provided you with lots of ideas; it might seem overwhelming. On the other hand, it might give you hope, encouragement. But start small. In part one, we focused on the physical. In part two, we will shift our focus to the emotional/energetic. As you begin your healing journey, try choosing at least one strategy from each area.

6

LIGHT BULB MOMENT

Is the anxiety that you are feeling even yours?

M y LIGHT BULB MOMENT was a defining moment with a client. One day, while working on a client, I kept being overwhelmed by negative, dark thoughts. They seemed to come out of nowhere, and no matter how many times I would push them away they would come back. These thoughts weren't part of my normal pattern of thinking even when I was feeling down or having anxiety. I thought to myself, "This is not like me!" I stopped for a second and then heard my own thought again, "This is not like me!" A HUGE lightbulb went off inside my head; I looked down at my client and realized it was THEM! Knowing this client and some of their struggles, I wasn't surprised they were having these thoughts. In that moment, I was able to separate myself from those thoughts, and I felt free! I then went back through my life, from the beginning of the anxiety, and was able to identify all the times I had been overwhelmed by *other people's* anxiety—it wasn't even mine! This was a VERY pivotal point for me. It was extremely liberating!

After this realization, I contemplated how, moving forward, I could determine if the anxiety was mine or someone else's. I came to the realization that, when the anxiety came on in waves that seemed to continually wash over me, no matter how many times I pushed it away, it was coming from someone else.

If this happens to you, it could be someone projecting their anxiety onto you or thinking of you while also thinking negative thoughts about their own life or about you. The anxiety can also be coming through in someone else's voice or energy. If the anxiety is in *your* voice and seems to align with the usual flow of your thoughts, then it is probably yours; then, you can trace it back to the worry and fear cycle that started it.

By the way, this doesn't just apply to anxiety; this experience can also help you understand, in general, when someone else is thinking of you.

Are You an Empath?

An empath can be described as a human sponge, soaking up the emotions of others. Quite often, an empath will also have gut issues (like celiac or other digestive sensitivities), because the gut holds on to emotions. (As an aside, sometimes childhood trauma is related to celiac that develops later in life.) For the empath, learning to set boundaries is so important! Otherwise, you go through life living everyone else's emotions *plus* your own, and it's exhausting. Read the boundaries section for more on this topic.

Suppressing Emotions

Sometimes, when you suppress *all* emotions, because you don't want to experience the one that feels like death (anxiety), you will also not recognize or allow excitement. In one case, when I was on my way to meet a friend and I was excited to go there, I realized I had some restriction of my breathing, and I felt anxious. I thought to myself, "What is going on here?" Then, I realized that I *was* actually excited to go but was confusing that feeling with anxiety. This is why it's important to stop and identify where the feelings are coming from.

You Can't Save Others

You are the only one you can do anything about. Being stressed about everyone else and embodying their problems doesn't help them *or* you. Having been raised to believe that others must be saved from hell, I had been conditioned to save others, to help others. A lot of energy is expended trying to save (change) the people around us. Similar to massage therapists or others in the holistic realm, we are apt to think that our approach or technique is the only right way and that other perspectives are wrong. But, there are so many different ways to get healthy. It's not selfish to live how you want. It's selfish to try to save (or change) others.

I know when I was really going through the anxiety, I did worse when people would sympathize with me, because it tends to invite a pity party. To this day, I will listen, give you space, and acknowledge you, but I will not sympathize. Often, in conversation, we are listening so that we can talk about ourselves, not listening to truly hear another. I've discovered over the years that most people aren't sharing their issue simply because they want another person's opinion; rather, they just want to be heard. That's it. Usually, after they've expressed themselves, they feel better. Once it's out in the air, it dissipates. And with most people, if you really listen to them, they already know what to do.

Looking back at my life, I can see that I was trying to save and help others because I needed to help and save myself. I have been there, and I can see all the warning signs of someone heading straight for burnout or some major health issue. I really want to tell them that if they continue their trajectory, it will lead to a not-so-good place. But I have realized that everyone is on their own journey. You can say what you want, but if they aren't at that place, ready to receive the information, nothing you can say will help them. And maybe you aren't the person to tell them.

Serving Others

The best way to get your mind off yourself and your pain is to help others. This is different from trying to *change* another. What I'm describing is being of service. What can you do to assist those around you? Babysitting, moving, volunteering? This is where you are genuinely helping, not trying to fix others or embody their emotions. You can still do this with boundaries.

Gratitude

Before I even understood what the word gratitude meant, and I was in the throes of the anxiety, I had gotten into the habit, while standing in the shower, of being grateful for three things. I found it would significantly help my mindset. "Thank you, thank you, thank you for the sunshine!" I don't remember the other two, but sunshine was one of them. Surprisingly, even though I was raised in a Christian home, I had not heard the word gratitude before, nor understood it.

Gratitude helps to lift you up out of pity, out of the lower vibrations of others and helps to stop the mind chatter—it literally interrupts the anxiety. Switching your thoughts from anxiety to gratitude might be challenging at first, but the more you do it, the easier it gets.

Gratitude can transform the anxiety in a moment, because you literally stop yourself mid-thought and ask, "What am I grateful for today?" It could be sunshine, a breath of fresh air, hot tea, freedom, or green lights. Your happy thoughts could also be happy memories. I would push away the thoughts that weren't serving me, with my hand, and then pull down an imaginary projector screen in my mind. On this screen would be one word of gratitude, and I would focus on that.

Gratitude...finding the good in what has happened in your life is HUGE! I am grateful for what I went through, because it made me who I am today, and I really like who I am.

Journaling

Get it out! The worry, the doubt, the fears, the good times, the bad times, the trauma, the sweet memories —why carry it around? Journal it out instead of having it swirl around and around in your brain. The time it takes to journal might seem like a commitment, but what is more important than your own health? What can you let go of that is NOT serving you (TV, scrolling on your phone, complaining to others, etc.)? How good would it feel to swap the negative for the positive?

Journaling can help you make better sense of what's going on. You can recognize patterns in your situation when you "see" it differently. I discovered a quick way to journal—instead of writing a whole story, write quick bullet points and/or write out a sentence or three, getting it out and then moving on. It's also helpful to scribe any memories that are haunting you or any unresolved matters. You can also write out what you'd like to forgive (or be forgiven for) and then burn it, freeze it, tear it up, or throw in the ocean, symbolic actions of release.

Get Excited About the Future

How do you wish to feel five years from now? When I needed encouragement, I would say to myself, "A year from now, I'll be so much better. Five years from now, I will have overcome this." In the grand scheme of things, a year or five years is so tiny and flies by quickly.

Don't plan your life around having anxiety forever. Find people who inspire you (in-person or online), and do what they do to feel better. Hint: quite often, those who have been on earth a while (forty-plus years) are those who have figured out that things will be ok...to not give a fuck...they understand how to say no, set boundaries, and ENJOY life! Don't let this condition cripple you—set your mind to overcome it!

Wouldn't you rather spend time envisioning a happy and healthy YOU than spend time figuring out how to live with anxiety? Sometimes, if you are feeling super anxious or nervous about a situation, remember that in a month from now, this will seem like no big deal. On your deathbed, what would you have wished you had done? Not given energy to? Said no to? Said yes to? Been honest or expressed yourself to? What would have *truly* mattered? Get super clear about what your life is all about. No apologies.

You Are Your Own Best Cheerleader

Encourage yourself as much as possible! Read uplifting or self-help books, watch funny videos, WATCH the movie *The Secret*, listen to music, engage in self-care, change your life, set boundaries, be You.

The Secret literally shifted my life, changed my direction, and gave me hope. When I watched this movie and Bob Proctor came on, it grabbed me! Two things resonated with me. First, the idea that I can change my DNA with my thoughts. At that time, I didn't like my DNA (where I came from), so that was an encouragement to me. And second, that society, government, and religion, don't really want you to know your full potential. *The Secret* and its profound truth so deeply resonated with me that I proceeded to watch it and listen to it over and over and over again. I would play it every day, because I desperately needed and wanted the words to penetrate my psyche and my soul...to shift me to a better place. I knew it would take time to deconstruct the foundation of my mindset, my attitude, similar to the excavation of a person's physical health. I distinctly recall saying to myself that in six months, my mindset will be a lot better.

I really didn't have a great support system while dealing with all the anxiety. I was pretty much on my own. Occasionally, I'd get some help from people who did not have the best intentions. But my determination was mine. I kept at it until, one day, I was able to look back and say, "Oh I *am* a lot better than a year ago. Oh, I am a lot better than two years ago. Oh, I feel a lot better than three years ago." After about five or six years, I was finally able to say, "Oh, it barely ever bothers me and, if it does, I know exactly where it comes from, and I can take care of it!"

Self-Reflection

1. Is your anxiety even yours? Can you decipher when it's yours versus someone else's? You might even be able to trace it back to your childhood or maybe in utero.
2. What can you do to encourage yourself? To be your best cheerleader? What can you do to get into a better mind space?
3. What was your lightbulb moment?
4. What are three things you are grateful for right now? See if you can grow the list each day, until you can easily name ten things you are grateful for.

7

HOLDING YOURSELF IN

As a teenager I loved music and wanted to be a rockstar. I remember the first moment I became aware of music; I was so fascinated by music that I bought three cassette tapes with my first allowance money. I also started writing song lyrics. I had a three-ring binder full of lyrics. When I had friends over, we would sing songs out of my three-ring binder together.

My desire to be a singer was shut down in a short time, because it was considered worldly, ungodly, not allowed in the church in which I was raised. I lied to myself at the conscious level, believing that I was ok with that decision. I kept listening to music, but I quickly learned not to vocalize, to not share my true desires or who I was, because none of it was allowed. Nobody truly cared about what I wanted. I unconsciously became resentful and angry, feelings that were constantly brewing under the surface. I had anger towards those who told me I couldn't use my voice throughout my teenage years and into my twenties, while ironically believing at the same time that I was ok with it.

Shortly after being told no, I got bronchial pneumonia. Once I recovered from that, I proceeded to have a cough every winter. I remember that it would start around Labor Day and go through the entirety of winter, until the end of April. I remember hearing that once you get pneumonia, you're more susceptible to getting it again. I thought to myself, "Not me! I am only going to get better. I'm not going to allow this to keep going on." So, I started to take different herbs, like mullein and garlic to help my lungs heal. Sure enough, every year the intensity of the coughing would get better and the duration shorter.

The very interesting part is that the moment I left the religion, removing myself from the religious abuse and narcissistic control, my coughing went completely away. That's because it was not a physical issue; it was all an emotional underlying suppression of my voice... who I am, and none of that was allowed. Restriction of my lungs, my voice, my throat. The moment I gave myself freedom, my lungs thanked me. Holding myself in for my own safety and protection, completely guarded, was my subconscious stance for years.

Holding Yourself In

Something I've noticed over the years with my massage clients is that some of them are on anxiety medication to suppress the true Self. They've never known how to handle their uniqueness, differentness, or special abilities (ie, psychic, medium, genius, or creativity). Sometimes, once you step outside of parental control or outside of the educational and peer control of college, you are finally able to THINK and FEEL FOR YOURSELF. There's this bubbling up to the surface of your true Self, and you often don't know how to handle it, because you were never taught how. So, instead, you submit yourself to the suppression and control of medication. But you are free now. What are you going to do?

When you try to suppress yourself, it can lead to anxiety. When you are caught up in fear or doubt, that is anxiety. Fear, worry, doubt, and indecision can lead to anxiety and depression. One of the best ways to give yourself hope is to make a decision...a "line in the sand" moment.

I remember going to a restaurant that was in an old, historic, psychiatric building, with bars still over some of the windows and certain wings blocked off. Prior to going to the restaurant, I didn't realize what the building had been. Once I learned what it was, I actually felt sick inside, because had I been alive back then, when they put you away for being crazy (aka, different), I'd probably have ended up there. I couldn't wait to get out of there, as the energy did not feel good!

Were you called a worrywart as a child? I was. It is really interesting that, as an adult, I can see where I was mirroring back the anxiety from others as a child. Children mirror and express out what they are around.

Intuition

Intuition...premonition...gut feeling. We all have it, sometimes saying we knew or saw something in our *mind's eye* or *third eye*. We may also call it a sixth sense, inspiration, an epiphany, a still, small voice, the holy spirit, the universe, perception, insight, or wisdom. These are all words/terms for the same thing. We may say things like, "I wonder" or "I feel like." This inner guidance is always leading you, nudging you, warning you. It's what picks up on red flags or another person's vibe (if they are angry or happy), and it's what gives you chills of fear. Most of us are looking for validation or guidance from others, when it is really inside each of us.

"You've had the power all along, my dear!" said the good witch from The Wizard of Oz.

Listen, listen, listen to it! Your intuition will tell you what to do and when to do it, where to go, what boundaries to set, what to eat, how much money to spend, what date to do something, when to text someone, when a person is lying to you...literally ALL THE THINGS! *The more you listen to it, acknowledge it, and follow it, the more it grows, and the truer your life will be.* You will no longer be a wide-open cup, allowing everything in to affect you, because you have a high-level filter to live by. You'll be glad you listened to it.

Being busy all the time will cancel out your intuition. You don't have to be busy or on-the-go all the time. Today, "busy" is a lifestyle, not an excuse. You *choose* to be busy, but quite often, this will prevent you from listening to your inner guidance. You will get better results, easier flow, and a calmer lifestyle when you are quiet, still, listening to yourself, and being led by your intuition. When you are so busy that you can't think or reflect on your life, the next thing you know, it is gone. You've worked or busied yourself to death.

They say we are so advanced these days—it's the technology that is advanced, not humans. Yes, humans created the technology, but it is meant to be a tool, not to run our lives. Try turning your phone off or on silent at night or take a digital detox day each week—I do all three of these and don't apologize.

The same thing applies with constantly taking pictures. I don't know how many times I would take a picture to share on social media and then delete it afterwards, because I knew I would never look at it again. The only photos I look at repeatedly are food pictures for my cookbook, some childhood photos of myself, pictures of family members, and photos of a few important events, like graduation. But all the sunsets, for example, are meant to be enjoyed in the moment.

Trust Your Intuition! Trust your gut. You are NOT crazy. The more you separate the anxiety from other conditions or factors, the more you are able to think and listen to your intuition. It can't talk to you if you are in a swirl of anxiety or listening to others instead.

Perhaps the anxiety is your intuition letting you know, in a very strong way, that what you are doing isn't working...that you're not safe. Hmmmm...if that might be the case, pay close attention to the last chapter of this book.

Forgiveness

Initially, the thought of forgiving...well, nobody really wants to hear it or do it. But once you understand how freeing it is for you and how quickly it speeds up your healing, it is totally worth it. And, it becomes easier to do. Because, yes, you'll be doing it more than once. Even though I was raised hearing about how Christ forgives sins, I had NO IDEA how to forgive others or myself. It was only through personal development that I learned how. What I've discovered along the healing path is that there can be layers to forgiving. You feel like you've let go of something but then another "thing" reveals itself about the same situation.

The first time I decided that I needed to forgive, in order to help me heal and move on, I put it off, danced around it, and had to get mentally prepared for it. One day, I just sat down and did it. I don't remember if I just spoke it out loud, said it in my head, or wrote it out. Over the years, I have written it out, while also speaking it out loud; then, I will typically either burn it or rip it up and throw it away.

Forgiveness is meant to set *you* free from the anger, the hurt, and the trauma that is keeping you from living freely. Don't worry about the other person—karma is a bitch and not your responsibility. Don't let them take up any more acreage in your mind.

I had a wise person say to me once, that how fast I heal is up to me. It could take five months or seven years to work through something; so, quite literally, you DO HAVE THE POWER TO HEAL yourself!

Here is my process for forgiveness:

It is what it is. Accept it. It happened. In order to forgive, you have to face it.

Realize the good from the situation. Extract the good.

Forgive the rest. When I first forgave, it felt weird. However, the more I practiced it, the more quickly I would start to recognize when it was time again, so I was able to forgive right away, rather than allowing a traumatizing or upsetting situation stick with me.

I also want to share this bit of wisdom for those experiencing grief from a heartbreak—know that the deep tears you have coming up wouldn't be there unless you had loved and loved deeply. To experience deep grief from a break up means you experienced an equally deep love, and for that, be deeply grateful.

Crying is a Release

For twenty-eight years, I was so tense! I had been holding myself back all those years, and I simply couldn't any longer. I was raised to think that crying was a weakness, so I rarely cried as a teenager or adult. I was often told not to cry or not to be like others who were always crying or miserable. But once the anxiety hit (the cracking open) it was like the dam that was holding back all the tears broke open. I cried for a year and half. I kept thinking, "What is wrong with me?" I would cry for no reason—anywhere! Then one day, I found myself so happy and grateful for something, that I started crying. In that moment, I realized that crying could be a good thing! It could express happiness, gratitude, love, grief, or just a release. That moment melted away the stigma of "bad" tears, and I started to distinguish the difference between them.

Let yourself cry; it's so cathartic!

Turn Off the TV and Go Outside

Stay away from the news. I still don't understand why it's so full of awful information. Why is that *the* news. It's more like drama and gossip. And they repeat themselves multiple times, telling you how awful life is and how awful humans are. I don't think we were meant to know about all the horrendous turmoil from around the world. Turn off the television, and go discover how amazing the earth is! Go on a walking meditation, where you walk to clear your mind. Notice the trees, nature, birds. State out loud ten things you are happy about or good things that happened that day. Keep walking until you feel better.

Dance

Dancing is an incredible form of exercise. It also helps to shake off any energy that is holding you down. Dancing loosens up all the joints, by increasing your circulation and giving you better motion—and motion is lotion (to the joints). In general, a lot of people have stuck energy in their pelvic area, even more so if you've had sexual trauma, landed hard on your tailbone, or given birth. If you've had trauma leading to feelings of unworthiness as a woman, it's also going to be stuck in the pelvis area. And this stuck energy can be relieved through dance. The more you dance and move your hips, the more you're going to energetically let the trauma go. How fun would it be to dance your way into feeling better?! Dancing and moving your hips will also help you feel more balanced in your feminine aspect, as that area is critical in keeping everything flowing well.

You also have your root (or base) chakra and your sacral chakra located in your pelvis area. Whether you're male or female, your root chakra has to do with worthiness, self-image, conditioning, family values, money mind-set...creating the foundation of who you are. The sacral chakra is all about creativity, sexuality, and feminine energy. If you think about it, a lot of creatives are not acknowledged, they are shut down, they're told they'll never make money with their art, music, cooking, sewing, etc.

At one point on my journey, I kept feeling like my tail-bone was bothering me, however, it didn't feel physical. I concluded that I had stuck energy in my pelvis. At the same time, I noticed I was fascinated by famous singers and their dance moves. I finally acknowledged that I had a deep desire to dance that was coming up to the surface. I was raised to believe that dancing or even moving your hips (gyrating) was not allowed, as it would make men notice and cause them to lust! I had discovered Zumba, a type of exercise dance, years earlier, and it had brought my desire back to the surface momentarily. Then, I heard about this dance for the chakras that was a freestyle, deeply meditative dance. After a few sessions of doing this dance, the stuck energy was gone. It made me aware of how important it is to move your hips, get in touch with yourself, and limber up your root and sacral chakras.

By the way, have you ever noticed that, when someone says something to you that you know doesn't belong in your orbit, you actually shudder or shake it off? That's because you immediately sensed it's not good for you. Your body knows what to do!

Reiki

Reiki is a technique that can be practiced with a light touch or no touch at all. Reiki is like a massage but for the energy fields around your body. It helps to clear your aura and align your chakras. Your chakras are the energy centers in your body. You actually have 183 chakras in your body, with the biggest ones on the bottoms of your feet; that's why grounding is so important and works so well. You might be familiar with the main seven chakras that run down the center of your body.

Reiki is also great for those who feel stuck on a plateau. This could be regarding fitness, food, relationships, money, mindset, or any number of things. A plateau feels like, no matter what you do, you can't break free to reach a higher level. When this happens, I suggest a different approach, through energy, instead of what you have been doing.

When looking for a Reiki practitioner, definitely go to someone you feel most drawn to (use that intuition). Asking for a word of mouth recommendation can also help you find a trustworthy practitioner. I knew I needed Reiki. When I first started receiving it, I didn't notice much until a few sessions in. It's an awakening to the energetic part of yourself that most of us aren't familiar with. We are so conditioned to focus on just the physical. If anything, you'll feel relaxed after the session. When I received my Reiki training, it changed my life by speeding up the healing journey and helping me understand the connection between the physical, emotional, and energetic bodies.

Self-Talk

Negative self-talk. I didn't realize the amount of negative self-talk I engaged in until, one day, I heard myself saying "That's so dumb!" Then, I realized how frequently I was saying it, which was a mindset I had picked up on in childhood. The things people say to themselves, or others, is a reflection of their own inner self-talk, and it's quite detrimental in the long run.

Have you ever heard yourself say things like:

"You might think I'm crazy..."

"I'll kill you!"

"This might not make sense to you..."

"I'm sorry..."

"What's wrong with you?"

"What's wrong with me?"

"Why can't I look like others?"

"The TV said I wasn't trendy."

"My ADHD is really acting up!"

These are all forms of negative self-talk. Think about changing the wording to:

"I've got this!"

"This is perfect timing!"

"I'm perfect just the way I am!"

Or, you could just share what you want to without a self-defeating disclaimer that puts yourself down.

When I talk about a healthy lifestyle, I also mean emotional health. Thoughts are nutrients too. If you looked at your thoughts, do you think health would grow from those? Is your self-talk full of self-hate, body shaming, and guilt? Or is it more gratitude for what your body does every day for you?

Mindset

I started investigating mindset and personal development to help my financial situation. Little did I know that it was everything *beneath the surface* that was contributing to financial lack. There was a lot more going on than I understood. When we have issues, we tend to be hyper-focused on improving that ONE thing. But usually, there are multiple factors contributing to the ONE thing and these other factors take care of themselves on the way to the bigger concern.

Mindset is similar to self-talk—do you stew on fears, doubts, and worries, or are you looking for the good in something that happened? Can you understand that a detour in life was purposeful to avoid further (or any) hurt? Evaluating your mindset and self-talk is hugely beneficial in evaluating where you stand in your own self-worth. When you see yourself without constant anxiety, would that person have high or low self-worth? How could that person get to being a better version of themselves?

It all starts with a decision and determination of the mind, and the mind controls the body. The body puts in the physical action to better health. Look at the mindset as the basement or foundation, the grassroots of who you are. Do you feel good building on top of a swamp or would you prefer firm, sturdy ground? You definitely want a good start, and that start can happen now. It's the little, consistent steps that lead up to the "big thing," and you can see the bigger changes as they add up. But you must start with the small steps, and you *must start*.

Choose your thoughts; spend time thinking about what you truly want. What DO you want to think about? What delights you the most to think about?

There is Nothing Wrong with You

Quite often, in the spiral of anxiety and "what is wrong with me" thinking, it is helpful to know that who you are is perfect—there is nothing wrong with you! Realizing that I was perfect just the way I was indicated a level of healing from the religious abuse.

Taking a personality test or knowing your zodiac sign (astrology version of personality traits) will help you to realize that who you are is just who you are! There is nothing wrong with you! Write out all the aspects of you that you LOVE. Yes, this is a self-help book on anxiety, but there is NO way I can let you finish this book without realizing that there is nothing wrong with you.

You are going through changes that are making you a *better* you. I am so glad I went through my struggle, because it made me who I am today, and I love who I am. Know that you ARE turning a corner into a better life. Sometimes, it takes a bit of time to get around the corner.

This is why it's so important to look at your anxiety and to dismantle it, so you can see all the shifts, changes, improvements, and healing. Otherwise, everything feels the same and stays the same. I know that I keep repeating this, but some of you are going to skip over this important realization, get the gist of the book, not purposely apply it, and then claim that it doesn't work.

Here are some of the ways that we are told that there is something wrong with us. Do any of these look or sound familiar?

You are a sinner, going to hell.

You're just a kid and don't know what you are talking about.

Nobody wants to listen to you.

Red marks on your school papers.

You never get it right.

There's something wrong with you.

Why can't you do it like a woman (complete emasculation)?

You're not popular.

You're not following the group, culture, skin color, style, or religions guidelines.

You are old.

You are too emotional or cry too much.

You are different. Why can't you be like the rest?

You're not perfect. (note: perfectionism is a form of control, which usually occurs as a coping mechanism due to trauma)

The reason I am spelling all of this out is because it's often so ingrained that we don't notice the reiterating message of, "something is wrong with you." When we compound all of those negative messages with child-hood trauma (physical, mental, spiritual, energetic), stress, the expectations of others, peer pressure in school, college or work stress, alcohol issues, injuries, heartbreak, a lack of nutrition or vitamins, or any other setback, it all compounds and snowballs into a bigger problem. And if ignored, it can lead to the body screaming at you for attention. If you habitually "man up" or push through it, it will either break you or cause you to finally listen to your intuition.

Self-Reflection

1. Notice over the next week what your self-talk is
   like. Would you want someone to talk to you
   like that?
2. Who do you know that you need to forgive? Do
   you need to forgive yourself?
3. How are you holding yourself in?
4. How have you been told that there is
   something wrong with you? Religion, culture,
   magazines, social media?

8

YOU CAN'T HEAL IN THE SAME ENVIRONMENT THAT YOU GOT SICK IN

You cannot heal in the same environment that you got sick in. When I first heard that, it hit with so much truth. Similarly, have you ever heard the saying, *you become just like the five people you hang around the most*? That can be hard to hear at first, as that means change...something different or new. This is especially difficult for those who like to blend in or who care what others think of them. If you want more of the same, that's easy. But obtaining something better requires a shift of some sort. Is what you are currently being "fed" truly for your good?

I once read an article explaining that if where you are isn't surrounded by loving people who want you to reach your fullest potential, then why are you there?

That was the moment I knew that I had to leave the religious church I was raised in, because the people within the church were so negative and purposely hurting each other. The amount of backstabbing, gossiping, putting others down, being better than others, hating, unforgiveness, doubting others' salvation, and judging stemmed from the illusion that we thought that who we were and what we preached was the best and only way. It was sickening when I really looked at it, and at that moment, I knew I was done. I only told one or two people I was leaving the church. I also decided to move away from the narcissistic control at the same time. I just stopped going to church and moved out on my own. In some ways I was shunned, but I didn't care. I was done, done, done! And since then, I have only moved forward. It has been a journey to heal the many layers of trauma, limiting beliefs, and anxiety, but it has been incredibly worth it!

I didn't realize the nature of narcissism until I left, because I was unknowingly breaking that chain, too. Not everyone's childhood story is the same. Actually, everyone's journey is different. You do what works best for you; know, also, that it's ok to change your mind. You can forgive a person, but that doesn't mean you have to trust them or ever be around them again.

In changing your environment, a primary point of focus is your home. But changes need to take place in yourself, as well. In this chapter, I discuss several ways to make your "dwelling" a true home, both physically and emotionally.

Negative Ions for Positive Energy

Both salt lamps and beeswax candles give off negative ions just like the ocean does, providing feel-good vibes and helping to purify the air, too. Additionally, salt lamps give off "fireplace feels" with their orange glow. For years, I had a big orange circle salt lamp in my massage room, and my clients would comment on how soothing the orange "moon" was. The salt lamps I am referring to are the ones with electric cords and light bulbs, not the stand-alone ones, because the electric lamps give off more vibration. Beeswax candles purify the air as opposed to paraffin candles that will release toxins into the room. Beeswax candles have a subtle honey smell.

Crystals

Crystals are like vitamins for your energetic being, your "soul." Every crystal has its own vibration/frequency/energy, and each one does its own thing. At first you might not notice anything when using crystals, but the more you use them, the more you'll notice how you feel with them and without them. They are excellent fidget gadgets, and these fidget stones have beneficial properties to them.

When I first started using crystals, I didn't notice they were working until, one day, when I *wasn't* carrying them. I suddenly realized that I felt better *with* them. One of the first crystals that I obtained was chrysocolla. I was drawn to the blue/green color and the fact that it helps with speaking your truth. I held it in my hand and closed my eyes. I felt this warmth travel up my arm and, in the very next moment, I sensed a metallic taste in my mouth. I knew, being in the holistic health field, that toxins coming out of my salivary glands taste like metal. My intuition spoke to me saying, "You've been swallowing other people's lies (toxins)." I knew that related to how I was raised. Such a profound moment!

Some crystals help to shift the environment, such as smoky quartz, flower agate, selenite, rose quartz, amethyst, lepidolite, and black obsidian and are great ones to start with. You can get them in a variety of shapes and sizes. Tumbled stones are the most common to start with. You can carry them in your purse, pocket, bra, or car, and you can fidget with them at the computer or while you are driving. You can put them in the underside of your pillowcase so you can receive energy while sleeping.

You can make your "place" a sacred space with crystals, one that feels so good to walk into...where you feel like a backpack has been removed from your back as soon as you step inside. How you do that is, first, set your intention for your home or space that you live in. Then, sage your home. Start by one side of your front door, sage your whole place, and end back at your front door (so it's one big circle). Lastly, put four rose quartz crystals in the four corners of your home for love and protection.

Boundaries, Boundaries, Boundaries

Setting boundaries! This is one that I have had to learn over and over again. As I have changed, my boundaries have had to change, too. They have actually gotten tighter as I get clearer and clearer about who I am and what I will allow in my life, because I get to have a say in my life. I refuse to be used or tossed about or sucked on by an energy vampire. Once you set your boundaries, DO NOT allow those who "use" your energy back into your life. Learn to say *no*; don't give them any additional information, be cautious, block them on social media, don't apologize, be matter of fact, and don't let them bully you.

Being a massage therapist, I've had to learn how to put boundaries around me, so I am not taking on my client's energy. It is not being unfeeling; it's being smart with my energy so that I can be an even better therapist. Besides, who wants a therapist with other people's energy being massaged all over them, too?

Even your phone needs boundaries. It'll be there, if you need it—it is a tool, not a life device. Turn it off at night or over the weekend. Have "business hours" with your phone, only look at it during certain hours, and only respond to people during certain hours. This will also help you to care less about what others think, because you aren't allowing them access to you every moment of the day. Notice if your anxiety seems worse after scrolling on social media. Being on the phone all the time, I do a phone detox every week. It is incredibly freeing.

There have been two times in my life where I didn't have enough money to pay for my cell phone, so it was disconnected. One time, it was for three weeks, and the other time was for three months. That was a huge eye opener for me! It showed me that the phone is a tool, not a life device. The phone is like an energy vampire.

When I first learned about boundaries and started to implement them, I first imagined that there was a long table that another person and I were sitting at. We were at opposite ends. Between the two of us, there was a glass wall so I could see and hear them, but all their words, energy, and actions stayed on their side; I didn't take them on. I practiced this visualization technique a lot with clients.

I honestly think that we, as a society, are too much in each other's business. Social media has made that very apparent. Social media is great for building a business but tends to tear apart personal life. I've noticed that, unfortunately, women are especially harsh to one another, instead of working to support and champion other women.

As you set boundaries, there may be some around you that won't like it. Especially, if you've decided to not be around those particular people as much. One way to ease the transition is to visit with them less often and stay a shorter amount of time. As you also heal and change, you may find that not all the people in your circle will support your growth. It can be sad, but do you want to keep the status quo or get better? Not only that, but by you choosing to heal, it may give them the courage to heal, too. You might not think of overcoming anxiety as a change or growth, but it will be. You wouldn't have sought out this book if you didn't want more for your life. You might not even realize how deeply your soul wants change. And lastly, when you change, it also helps to separate those who truly support you from those who enjoyed your suffering.

Try using a white light of protection. Imagine a white bubble around you, protecting you. In that white bubble, it is bright and sunny and positive. You have the ability to protect yourself with your intentions, instead of being a sponge or dumpsite for others. Before you go into any situation, you can imagine this white light around you, and anything they say will be reflected off the bubble.

Learn to think for yourself. Whenever I experienced a difficulty or was going through a major change, I always found myself pulling away from all those who thought they knew what I should be doing with my life. Now, I only listen to me, my intuition, and my inner guidance. It's very helpful to stop the noise of other voices and just listen to your own.

I had a reading by a medium once and was told that my empathic intuitiveness is SOOO strong that I can look at an object and know the whole history of it. I can even do that with people, at times, but I have boundaries up to protect myself, so I am not being dragged down by others or living their life energetically. From now on, I only want to live my life. I've done it the other way for too long.

What you think of me is none of my business; rather, it's your problem (karma).

Please Enjoy the Music

MUSIC can change your mood. Find a song you can hang on to whenever you feel hopeless...perhaps you already have one. Listen to relaxing piano music that calms your spirit, soothes your soul, and lulls you to sleep.

Music is one of the quickest and easiest ways for the universe to talk to you. Have you ever noticed how a song will come on that just "happens" to be right on target for what you are feeling and going through at that time? The next time you listen to the music playing (even in the stores), pay attention. It's one of the quickest ways to uplift your soul. The vibration of music is powerful. You might be hearing and feeling the beat of a familiar tune, but pay close attention to the words.

Music is one of the areas in our life where we are 100 percent allowed to feel all the emotions and express them, judgment free. It's also something you can do very easily for yourself. Plus, you can listen to music while doing other things, and it's cheap!

Did you know that whistling, singing, clapping, or snapping your fingers are some of the quickest ways to shift the energy around you? There have been times when I literally have had to say *no* to negative energy coming my way while snapping my fingers three times to stop it.

A sound bath is literally where you lay down on a yoga mat and let the music that is played wash over your body. It is very meditative, therapeutic, shifting, and incredibly relaxing. You may be able to find a sound bath facilitator in your area or listen to one online.

Do It For YOU

Ultimately, this is your journey. Others can help, but this path is yours and you get to make it whatever you desire.

Make sure you are doing what sets your soul on fire!

Whatever helps you feel calm in a healthy manner...do that over and over again.

The Crutch

A crutch is anything that we rely on that prevents us from operating from within our own power and ability. A crutch can be necessary in the short-term, as we strengthen and heal, but relying on a crutch long-term can have a negative impact...it stunts our growth. Sometimes we lean on people as a crutch. Perhaps you lean on someone to go places with you, in case you don't feel well. I have been there. It's a safety net, just in case. At some point you won't want it anymore, which is a sign of healing. I felt bad for using people as an "emotional support animal," even though it helped. But I realized I was essentially an energy vampire on them.

Down or Depressed

With anxiety, you might also feel down or depressed, to a degree, especially initially. When I first experienced anxiety, I did feel down; I felt like I was being sucked into a dark hole. That was my line in the sand moment...when I decided that was NOT going to continue. Whenever I've felt myself being suppressed, in any way, or not allowed to be ALL of myself, I get a little down. But suppression will do just that.

In a way, being down or depressed is a combination of hopelessness, "what is wrong with me" thinking, not living *on purpose*, and a need for hormonal support.

How Long Will It Take?

It was about six years along my journey when I realized, one day, that I wasn't controlled by the anxiety anymore and, if it did crop up, it was momentary. You probably want someone to tell you exactly when it will all be gone. Well, it's different for each person. At some point, you'll be able to see how the feeling of anxiety is less and less. Then one day you'll realize it is gone. The buckets overflow with calmness and, one day, you'll just realize that you've done it! You'll feel free, calm, and peaceful—it has to happen, I do know that.

When you first start out on your healing journey, it can seem overwhelming at first, like there is a lot to process. Yes, there is a lot to work through, but keep going. At year one, you'll look back and think, "Wow, I made progress!" By year two, you'll know you've made even more progress, and what you have to work through might lighten up a bit. By the time you get into year three to year five, somewhere in there, there will be much less you have to work through, and you'll be able to process it faster and easier. There will also be more clarity of mind. Bookmark this page so you are reminded over and over again that you WILL overcome.

That Person That Truly Sees You

When I entered my 30s, I had someone come into my life, for the first time, that truly believed in me. I was unconditionally supported, encouraged, safe, and allowed to be vulnerable. By seeing myself through their eyes, it helped me to see myself that same way. This stark contrast of the rest of my life gave me hindsight to realize what was true, what were lies, and who I deeply knew myself to be. When you are being lied to or controlled, it's all you know; you don't know anything different. But the moment you see the truth, you are given hope that you didn't know you needed. It is truly life-changing. Words and thoughts are powerful energy.

Sometimes, your bravery is felt by others, before you feel it—others have to mirror back to you your true essence before you, yourself, understand your beauty and strength, gifts that you've had all along. When someone believes in you, and holds space for you to save yourself, it is a true gift. They might not even realize that they did this for you.

If you are in a loving relationship, one of the best ways to help heal in any situation is to let yourself be loved.

Love heals. Let it lift you up...float on that high, trust the love. If you are experiencing it now, then let it serve its purpose.

Sometimes the universe will send a baby or some other form of love to help soften the situation, to comfort you, to help you heal, or to overcome a loss. Usually, the baby or love will save you, enabling you to get through a difficult time.

Water

Water will shift you. It's one of the reasons we are so drawn to water, and it comes in many forms: rivers, lakes, creeks, ponds, oceans, waterfalls, and even snow, as that is water, too. Why is water so healing? Because we are mostly water ourselves. It's why people gravitate towards the beach for vacation—it renews and relaxes them. It's also why drinking water helps the body to vibrate at a higher level. It's why enemas and colonics are also uplifting...a person feels lighter from the immediate water fusion. Water is meditative. Have you ever noticed how, after a long work day, showering feels SO GOOD? It's more than dirt you are washing off; it's the energy of your work environment, too.

Fire

Lighting a match can shift negative vibrations. Standing around a bonfire can feel so warming, so grounding... like it's shedding layers. There's also something about a fireplace that induces comfort and connection. Those sitting around a fire usually have great conversations. It can also serve as white noise, in a way, where it blocks out other sounds and energies. Fire, just like water, is meditative.

If you love candles, they are associated with being home and can help you shift from work to home. Quite often, it is the energy of candles, the flame, the fire element that is shifting your energy. You know this information on an unconscious level. So, it may manifest on the conscious level as an affinity for candles. It might even seem like an obsession. It may just be your desperate need to let go and shift your energy, and candles might be the only way you are allowing these shifts.

Self-Reflection

1. What boundaries do you need to set?
2. Who is that person in your life who gets you and supports you unconditionally?
3. How can you improve your environment so you can fully heal?
4. How does dance and music show up in your life?

9

PLEASE JUST LAUGH

Going through trauma, healing, and being overwhelmed by anxiety can all feel SOOOO SERIOUS and exhausting!

Please. Just. Laugh!

Laughter is good medicine and very healing. Are you laughing and smiling enough? I would watch all the "I Love Lucy" episodes to help lift me out of the downward spiral. This meant so much to me that I hung pictures of Lucy laughing in the gluten-free bakery and juice bar that I operated. To this day, I greatly treasure good-hearted humor and laughter.

Laughter is Medicine

Laugher is actually an orgasm for the belly, and if you pay close attention, you might even be able to notice that you feel the same area of your belly tighten (under your navel) as when you have a sexual orgasm. (At least for the ladies.) You might also notice that after experiencing sexual pleasure, whether with a partner or yourself, you feel like giggling or laughing afterwards; that's because it's activating that same area in your lower belly. It is all related.

Laughter induces the feel-good hormones. Laugher's happy juju lifts you up and dispels the blues. Whatever encourages you to laugh is really important. The vibration of laughter also helps to shift your whole being—physical, energetic, and emotional—as well as your aura (the light that your body gives off energetically). Your laughter also helps to uplift others.

I remember, as a child, laying in a circle with friends, where one kid put the back of his head on the next kid's belly. Then, the first kid would say "ha," the second kid would say "ha, ha," the third kid would say "ha, ha, ha," and so on, their "ha's" representing where they were within the circle. The idea was to see how many ha's could be said before someone in the circle would start laughing. It was a hilarious game, full of joy and laughter.

When you laugh, the world just seems brighter!

PLEASE.
JUST.
LAUGH!

P.S. ENJOY YOUR LIFE, and be your unique self (no two snowflakes are the same; no two fingerprints are the same). Who you are doesn't need any validation from others. Trust your own inner guidance. Living *your own* best life is the most important thing!

Self-Reflection

1. What makes you laugh?
2. How can you incorporate laughter into your daily life?

10

ANXIETY IN A NUTSHELL

This last chapter is a testament to how writing can be especially healing. During the process of writing this book, I had another major lightbulb moment—a clearer understanding of what anxiety truly is.

As you can see from this book, there are many different things that can cause anxiety. So, that got me thinking... is anxiety the issue? Or, are we so focused on anxiety that we aren't seeing what is truly going on? What is really behind anxiety? What is the anxiety really telling us? In other words, anxiety is the warning bell, the red-light indicator, the red flag, the siren, the dust storm in your face, indicating that something is not working. It's our intuition working overtime to let us know that something is OFF! The "symptom" of anxiety tells us that our body needs attention...that something or someone is affecting us emotionally...that we are unsafe. It's notifying us that energetically, we are a wide-open cup, receiving everything with no boundaries.

Anxiety is a Messenger

There is nothing "wrong" with anxiety, per se. Similar to a shiver or getting the goosebumps, it's your body sending you a message; for example, that you are cold... put on some warmer clothes. Same thing with anxiety —when it shows up, ask yourself, "What is this telling me?" And then, act accordingly.

We are so busy numbing out the *messenger* of anxiety, that we aren't listening for the message! Don't be annoyed or mad at the messenger; pay attention to the message. It's like being so concerned about acne or dark circles under the eyes, that we totally miss the fact that the skin is merely a messenger, a mirror from the body telling us that something is off inside.

For me, the panic attack was a "breaking open." It was my intuition saying, "You are not safe. This is not working for you."

Let's talk about how fear, anxiety, and nervousness all show up. In the case of a fear of flying, for example, you know that you have it, and it's a specific fear or phobia. Anxiety, on the other hand, is letting you know that something is off (internally or externally). Nervousness is more situational and temporary, like when you are giving a presentation, performing in a recital, or taking an exam. It shows up as butterflies in the stomach, sweating, having no appetite, and so forth. Once you engage in the activity, though, you usually start to feel better...you go into automatic pilot and accomplish the "thing."

Again, understanding helps to dissipate the control that fear, anxiety or nervousness has over you.

You're free!

Self-Reflection

1. How do you numb out the anxiety in order to ignore what it is telling you?
2. What is anxiety telling you?

Have I Overcome Anxiety?

Have I, personally, overcome anxiety? Well, to be honest, I thought I had overcome it. I would occasionally experience anxiety but quickly realize where it was coming from or who it was coming through. Then, I would either work through it, or it would dissipate on its own, once I had identified it. I was doing really well for years, but then, I taxed myself out, and the anxiety showed up again, in full force. Our physical health definitely affects our emotional health. One stressful year took a toll on me. Once I felt safe, my body let me know that it was TIRED of keeping me going.

Out of nowhere, I was experiencing anxiety again; I started feeling like I was out of breath. I thought, "Oh, I just ended my period, so I must be low on oxygen. I just need some chlorophyll." Then, that episode spiraled into full blown anxiety...feeling stuck. It reminded me of my anxiety when it was at its full-blown peak many years earlier. I thought to myself, "What is going on here?"

When you are super stressed out, sometimes you don't realize how stressed you are—you might be in survival mode or have tunnel vision—until you are no longer dealing with the source of the stress; then it hits your body with a *bam*! I realized my adrenal glands had been greatly taxed the year prior, and they were needing some relief.

I knew I had to get on it quickly, so I did everything that I knew had helped me before. I didn't waste any time: liver cleanses, reiki, massage, chiropractor, adrenal support, L-lysine, rosemary, blood building (vitamin E, chlorophyll, blackstrap molasses), enemas, probiotics, getting outside and walking, gratitude, meditation, examining my life and career, working through resentment towards massage, protecting myself from clients' energy, resting, healing of residual trauma, and stepping fully into my true creative Self.

This particular episode lasted about three months, until I did the liver cleanse. The liver cleanses that I did really flipped the switch for me. It took the anxiety way down to less than 20 percent.

The Reiki sessions that I received also helped shift me energetically. I was reminded that I was taking on too much of my massage clients' energy, and I needed to have better protection, better boundaries. It felt very much like the Epstein-Barr was in its active attack stage; it hit me out of nowhere...feeling chilled, having fevers, and being anxious.

I was reminded that life gets to be really, really good. I was reminded to choose my thoughts wisely...that I was not living within in my passion or speaking my voice.

This was a huge reminder of how much the physical body can affect the emotional. Sometimes, you just focus on the emotional on your healing journey. But as I mentioned earlier, the physical plane is typically the last focus of healing.

Now that some time has passed, and I have done A LOT more healing with regard to the closing out of old trauma and the breaking of chains, I can see that the anxiety spell that I had was both a physical stress response and an emotional/energetic hold. It's interesting that, as I worked through this book, I would get really tired and yawn a lot. This told me that I was working through some old wounding, pushing through it by giving voice to who I am through my writing. I can tell that some residual, but minimal, emotional healing is on its way out the door. It has been completely worth it!

With the original years-long healing, there wasn't any particular thing that was "the" miraculous healing moment; rather, it was a collective of methods that helped me overcome my anxiety in the long run. This most recent episode, though, was greatly helped by the liver cleanse and stepping into my creative self.

P.S.
There is
NOTHING
Wrong with You

ACKNOWLEDGMENTS

Allison and Will Brown at Palm and Lotus Publishing - Thank you for being incredible lightworkers and sharing the publishing opportunity in an honest, transparent, and wholesome way. I greatly appreciate your guidance.

Samantha - Thank you for your meticulous editing skills and joy! Thank you for understanding the spirit of this book.

Dr. Gillespie - Thank you for sharing with the world the technique you developed, The Gillespie Approach. There are so many happy adults from your commitment to having happy babies!

Dr Patton - Thank you for the endless holistic training, herbal knowledge, and wisdom that you have shared. You have helped to heal countless numbers of people who had no one else to turn to.

Frank - Thank you for being "the one that got me" and your support. Thank you for giving me a different perspective on life, which changed the direction I was going in, and ultimately, helped me to see a better version of myself.

Herbert N. Nunag (NHawk) at 99 Designs - Thank you for the amazing cover design!

Myself - I thank myself for determining years ago to overcome anxiety and heal myself and for having the courage to write this book and share my voice.

ABOUT THE AUTHOR

Aura Jaddee is an expert in the holistic health field, having helped thousands of folks lead healthier, happier lives. Aura is a Licensed Massage Therapist, Licensed Esthetician, Colon Hydro-therapist, and Reiki Practitioner, as well as being Lymphedema Certified. After over twenty years in "the field," owning her own spa, gluten-free bakery and juice bar, and training under the direct supervision of a Naturopathic Doctor, Aura is ready to share, with others, the wealth of knowledge she's learned along the way.

To connect with Aura, please email her at:

loveintuitiveliving@gmail.com

RESOURCES

Aura's truest desire is to provide resources that help people to live in their fullest potential, being guided by their intuition. To that end, she has created a wellness resource hub that houses multiple offerings: self-care products, an herbal apothecary, books, gluten-free baked goods, oracle card decks, gifts, and more!

Website/Etsy shop:

www.etsy.com/shop/loveintuitiveliving

Learn:

To learn more about your fascinating fascia, Dr Barry Gillespie, & The Gillespie Approach visit:

www.gillespieapproach.com

Shop:

For Essential Oils – check out as my guest:

https://referral.doterra.me/959884

For self-care products, herbal teas, herbal tinctures, guides for enemas/colonics and liver cleansing, and more:

www.etsy.com/shop/loveintuitiveliving

Social Media:

www.instagram.com/in.tuitiveliving

www.tiktok.com/@in.tuitiveliving

www.youtube.com/@intuitivelifestyle

www.pinterest.com/infointuitiveliving